MW01156891

the
ONE PAN
galley gourmet

simple
cooking
on boats

by **DON JACOBSON**
& **JOHN ROBERTS**

International Marine / McGraw-Hill

Camden, Maine • New York • Chicago • San Francisco • Lisbon • London •
Madrid • Mexico City • Milan • New Delhi • San Juan • Seoul • Singapore •
Sydney • Toronto

The **McGraw·Hill** Companies

9 10 11 12 13 14 15 16 17 18 19 DOC DOC 15

© 2004 International Marine

Library of Congress Cataloging-in-Publication Data
Jacobson, Donald.
  The one pan galley gourmet : simple cooking on boats / Don Jacobson
and John Roberts.—1st ed.
     p.   cm.
Includes index.
  ISBN 0-07-142382-6
  1. Cookery, Marine. I. Roberts, John, 1938– II. Title.
  TX840.M7J33 2004
  641.5'753—dc22   2003021411

Questions regarding the content of this book should be addressed to
International Marine
P.O. Box 220
Camden, ME 04843
www.internationalmarine.com

Questions regarding the ordering of this book should be addressed to
The McGraw-Hill Companies
Customer Service Department
P.O. Box 547
Blacklick, OH 43304
Retail customers: 1-800-262-4729
Bookstores: 1-800-722-4726

Photographs by the authors.

Contents

Acknowledgments

We would like to thank the many people who have contributed to this cookbook, in some cases by sharing their own recipes with us but more often by trying out the recipes on these pages and then offering their feedback.

In addition, there are two people who deserve special mention. To Don's wife Pam, who has always encouraged him to create new, nonmicrowave recipes for their table, we express our deepest gratitude. She not only brings a sense of adventure to their kitchen but her professional expertise has helped make these offerings more nutritious and healthful. We extend a similarly heartfelt sense of gratitude to John's wife Susan, who always found ways to create delicious meals on two burners during six years of cruising with a galley whose floor space totaled barely more than 2 square feet. Susan's common galley sense has done much to help us keep our culinary ambitions afloat realistic.

Introduction

This book had its origins in the wilderness. Don is an avid backpacker who also enjoys eating. He didn't really want to boil water when setting up his nighttime campsite so that he could "feast on a freeze-dried brick called Chicken Gumbo."

Instead, he wanted, in his words "something fresh, with crisp green vegetables, a succulent sauce, and that toothsome, satisfying, filling feeling only real food can give. Perhaps a nice dessert. Something to be savored, not tolerated. Something that encourages companions to linger over the evening meal and the ensuing conversation. Something that soothes the digestion, improves your outlook, chases away the gloom of an unwelcome rainstorm, and requires a lot less water to prepare than the freeze-dried alternatives."

The result was *The One Pan Gourmet*, a cookbook that has tantalized the taste buds of thousands and thousands of campers since it was first published in 1993.

Although *The One Pan Gourmet* was written initially for backpackers, it could just as well have been written for cruisers. After all, we mariners deal with many of the same issues. We get tired of eating out of cans. Most of us have only one or two burners on our stoves. We may or may not have an oven and, if so, it's usually a small one at best. Most of us don't have automatic dishwashers or an endless supply of water on our boats, so we too are concerned about not having a bunch of dirty pots and pans to clean up. Moreover, even though we don't have to find dead branches and break up wood to make a campfire for cooking or carry a camp stove with its fuel on our backs, we do try to conserve our stove fuel. And finally, most of us enjoy eating good food—even gourmet meals!

What this means, of course, is that many if not most of us who go out for weekends, weeks, months, or even years to cruise on small boats are always on the lookout for good recipes for one-pot meals—that is, meals that are both a pleasure to eat and can be prepared using only one cook pot or frying pan.

Now, here's the good news. With this cookbook, we're in luck. The *One Pan Galley Gourmet* has been revised from its original focus to put the cruising yachtsman at the forefront. It includes new recipes and it will complement almost every galley. This means that whether your boat's food-keeping and cooking facilities are only minimally more sophisticated than the backpacks and camp-fires with which most of these recipes were perfected, or you are lucky enough to have refrigeration, a three-burner stove with built-in oven and a microwave, or your galley facilities lie somewhere between those two extremes, there's a wealth of good eating for you in these pages.

Creating, borrowing, testing, fine-tuning, personally enjoying, and then field-testing and receiving feedback about these recipes has taught us what per-sonal expressions cooking and eating are. Our biases and preferences are re-flected throughout this book—it could be no other way. For example, we are fussy enough about cooking oils to carry four kinds (vegetable, olive, peanut, and corn) if the menu calls for them. Moreover, we're omnivores. A mix of meat and veggies not only makes a balanced and healthy diet, it also makes for some in-teresting food opportunities. In addition to the meat-driven items, you'll find some delicious vegetarian recipes; the Oven chapter has a section called Vege-tarian Delights (see pages 144–50), but other chapters have meatless dishes as well. Or you can adapt many recipes by simply leaving out the meat. The index will help you find anything you're looking for. The meat substitution ideas and the protein complementation chart on pages 26–27 reinforce the fact that cruis-ing adventures and vegetarianism need not be incompatible. In fact, they can fit together quite nicely.

Turning to the recipes, unless otherwise noted they serve two average peo-ple average portions. If you're cooking only for one person, you can adjust most of the recipes simply by halving the main ingredients and cutting back somewhat on the spices. The same logic, but in reverse, applies when cooking for more than two (or for two very hungry people!). In general, increase the portions by 50 percent for three people. For four, double the portions—unless, of course, those third and fourth people are teenagers whose appetites may demand a bit more. You can also always bump up the vegetables, sauces, and side dishes to help satisfy larger appetites. But when scaling up to feed more people, be careful to increase the spices only sparingly.

The cookware recommended in the Cruising Galley chapter will feed one or two, but for larger groups you'll want a larger (12-inch) frying pan. Depending upon what you're using for an oven, it may not suffice for larger groups; you could cook the meat portions in it, but you may not have room for the vegetables.

Finally, just as in many other endeavors, there's probably nothing in cooking that hasn't been tried a thousand times before. And we tip our collective culinary hats to all those enterprising cooks who, over the years, have tried to brighten the insides of their friends, families, and neighbors.

The reader, especially an experienced cook, will find that many of the recipes on these pages are old favorites presented with a slight twist. And that's the intent of this little work—to give new life to cruising cuisine.

Bon appetit!

a Philosophy of Cooking

It seems there are two approaches to eating on a small cruising boat (by "small," we mean any boat measuring from about 18 to about 40 feet). The first approach is represented by advocates of keeping everything simple, which more often than not means eating largely out of cans or packages. The other is the "hot-food-at-every-meal" philosophy, regardless of weather or sea conditions.

Frankly, we find neither one of these approaches appealing. The notion of eating out of cans is OK if there's no other choice (in the midst of a gale, for example). But going to sea armed with a can opener and a spoon is simply unacceptable under normal cruising conditions as far as we're concerned. And that holds whether we're cruising for a weekend, a week, or a year.

The proponents of keeping it simple say that the cook should spend as little time in the galley as possible. And we can understand that. After all, the gastronomic pleasures from eating Beefaroni and canned green beans aren't worth much time spent in the galley. On the other hand, the mouthwatering enjoyment of dining on Beefy, Cheesy Elbows (see recipe on page 116) is worth every bit of the 20 to 30 minutes it takes in the galley to prepare it.

As for the "hot-food-at-every-meal" ideal, it strikes us that stories we've heard or read of hardy seagoing cooks who produce hearty, hot, three-course belly-busters as their 38-foot sloops race through a gale with a triple-reefed main and a storm jib are simply that—sea stories.

Moreover, from a practical perspective, trying to turn out a hot meal under adverse sea conditions—even including lying to anchor in a choppy, windswept anchorage—is not at all appealing. With the boat being tossed, rolled, and slapped by waves, trying to cook and serve hot food—not to mention trying to eat it—can be downright dangerous. And we've got the burn scars to prove it.

So we need to look at galley cooking another way.

This epicurean philosophy starts with the fact that we like to eat good food— food that earns the cook compliments and, as suggested previously, food that is so delicious to eat that the pleasure it gives makes every minute spent in its preparation worthwhile.

It also means using fresh food whenever possible. Added to that is a preference for keeping cleanup easy, which most often means using only one pot (or pan).

Our preference for fresh meats, vegetables, and fruits on board is not as unrealistic as it may appear at first glance. Most people spend a major part of their cruising time either at anchor within dinghy distance of a grocery store or in a marina, where transportation to the store is readily available.

Moreover, when we're away from a source of fresh foods, usually it is for only a few days to a week—in other words, a short enough time that we can usually stock up on fresh foods to carry us through those days. If, in the end, we need to dip into our canned reserves, that's fine. But even then a little creativity and planning ahead will enable us to do a lot better than eating straight from a can.

DIET AT HOME . . . EAT ON YOUR BOAT

You need calories when you are on the water. Think about it for a minute. The boat is always moving—maybe only a little, but it is moving. And every time the boat moves, your body moves to adjust for the boat's motion. Your muscles are in action constantly. Which means that you are working constantly—even when you're just sitting there. And even when you're sleeping. That's one reason people usually find that their appetites seem larger on the water.

This means that you should plan for three hearty meals a day plus plenty of snacks. A good breakfast will get you up and going faster than any splash of seawater and will keep you going longer. Lunch can be a little lighter if you want, but try to hit the four basic food groups.

Fruit can have a special role. Apples, pears, and peaches are Mother Nature's no-need-to-cook, ready-to-eat, tasty convenience foods. They're also healthy, something you can't say for most prepackaged snacks. If you'll be away from civilization for too long to keep the fruit fresh, dried apricots, peaches, apples, and plums (we used to call them prunes!) make great snacks as long as you don't eat them all in one day.

Then there's dinner. The end of the day. Watching the sun set from your cockpit while dining alfresco.

Fill the crew's plates—and thus their stomachs—with deliciously prepared fresh food, and the planets will align and the music of the heavenly spheres will accompany the setting sun.

Cooking for nourishment, though, can and should be fun. Time spent in the galley should be just as rewarding as time spent in the cockpit, at the helm, or in any other activity on the boat. And a major part of galley time ought to involve food preparation. As far as we're concerned, it's not drudgery to add freshly sliced veggies to a broth simmering around a couple of succulent chops. In fact we savor those moments as much as a scenic anchorage graced by the widespread wings of a heron.

Moreover, you need not be bent over the stove continuously for two or three hours. Good food should be left to itself, to blend its flavors and to work its magic in secret. With the prep work out of the way and the food in the pot, pan, or oven, there is time to take a few minutes to get organized for dinner. To clean up. Read. Enjoy a refreshing drink in the cockpit. Or grab your camera to capture the sights around you.

And when the kitchen timer goes off to tell you that your creation has finished cooking, you can sit down to your dinner and eat the way the French do—taking your time, digging into something that is really worth enjoying, and appreciating the fact that you cooked it. What you are doing, of course, is paying yourself the ultimate compliment: that you do deserve to live well.

the
Cruising Galley

With fresh, clean air filling your nostrils and a rich blue sky dotted with white puffballs or wispy horsetails above your anchorage, you should be able to enjoy the aromas and tastes of your creations in a galley environment that is as relaxing as the surroundings.

That means that you—the cruising chef as opposed to the ship's cook—need a galley that lets you pursue your culinary quests without frustration or long hours down below while others are relaxing in the cockpit or cooling off with a quick dip. That also means having the right equipment in your galley.

If your boat is equipped with a full galley—defined here as one with a refrigerator or icebox, a two- or three-burner stove with oven, and stowage space for pots, pans, dishes, glassware, etc.—you can enjoy the luxury of having a full range of kitchenware on your boat. Then, after your first season of following the one-pan cooking philosophy, you can have the even greater pleasure of taking all the utensils and cooking equipment that you haven't used that year off the boat.

If, however, your boat is more modest, you are equally blessed because you really need only one frying pan and/or a one- or two-quart pot to enjoy roughly two-thirds of the recipes in this gourmet cookbook. Moreover, if you want an oven, you can have a stovetop oven simply by carrying one more item roughly the size of your frying pan or, at worst, the size of a large pot.

Finally, if you plan the menu for your cruise ahead of time, you need to take cooking gear for only the meals you've planned. It can be all frying pan, all pot, all stovetop oven, or any combination of the three.

THE GALLEY STOVE

Boat stoves range from one-burner units to two- or three-burner gimballed stoves with a built-in oven. Fuel for the stove can be butane, propane, alcohol, or kerosene. We've seen (but not tried) stovetop units with both electric heating

The galley on an Albin 30 family motorcruiser. Note the Glowmate butane stove plus a microwave and refrigerator.

A Glowmate butane stove on a 26-foot Cobalt motorboat. An adapter ring fits on the burner to keep the pot in place. The stove stows in the locker beneath the countertop.

elements for use with shore power at the marina and alcohol burners for when you're under way or at anchor.

Any of these stoves will cook your food, but we vote for butane or propane as a first choice because they have an instant and clean hot flame. If you have a pressure-alcohol stove, we suggest replacing it for safety reasons. Too many galley fires have been started when things went awry while trying to preheat the stove's burners.

If you want to stay with alcohol, a nonpressurized alcohol stove such as the Origo one- or two-burner stove is infinitely safer than the pressurized alcohol systems of old. But if you're going to replace that old stove, consider switching to propane or butane. The alcohol flame is not nearly as hot as a gas flame, so everything takes longer to cook. And that, of course, means more time you have to spend in the galley.

Kerosene is a completely different animal. John's boat, *Sea Sparrow*, has a two-burner pressure-kerosene stove and oven that has done yeoman's service for more than twenty years and well over thirty thousand cruising miles, both inshore and offshore. The safety issue of preheating the kerosene burners is eliminated by using a wick to contain the alcohol in the preheating cup, but few people want the extra work involved. And besides, propane and butane are much easier and cleaner to use.

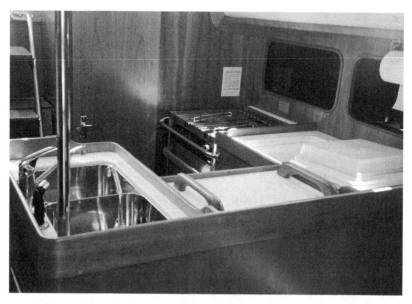

The galley on this J-42 has a three-burner propane stove with a built-in oven. Note the top-opening icebox and double sink.

An Origo wick alcohol stove in the galley of a Corsair F-27 trimaran.

OVENS

You can enjoy the mouthwatering food cooked in an oven even if your stove does not have a built-in unit. How? By using a stovetop oven.

Stovetop ovens work just as well as built-in ovens, but they do have limitations. For example, you can't cook a standing rib roast in a stovetop oven. But then again, you can't cook one in most of the ovens built into the stoves on small boats, either; they're far too little. So compared with most small-boat ovens, the limitations are modest.

One stovetop oven that a cruiser can borrow from the world of camping is the

The diffuser plate and ring base on a stove burner.

Outback Oven (call Backpackers Pantry at 303-581-0518 or go to www.backpackers pantry.com). It consists of (1) a bottom metal plate designed to radiate heat from the stove's burner into the "oven" and to diffuse the heat evenly over the bottom of the pan; (2) a low ring-stand whose three legs fit into a bottom plate to support the oven about $1/2$ inch above the plate; (3) a nonstick 10-inch frying pan with a domed lid and without a handle; (4) a thermometer that is screwed onto the top of the lid; and (5) a collapsible "tent" made of a heavy, tightly woven fiberglass fabric that is aluminized on the inside to reflect heat back toward the pan.

Base and oven pan and lid on the stove burner.

Complete oven assembly on the stove burner. Note that the tent is held above the burner level.

The oven disassembled for stowage. A net bag that comes with the unit is not shown.

The potgrabs used to lift the hot pan.

In essence, the covered pan is the cooking dish. The fiberglass hood serves as the sides and top of the "oven," so the covered pan is heated from all sides. The entire unit stows in a box measuring 3 inches high and about 10 inches square. Assembled, the top of the pan's lid is barely 4 inches above the burner. The thermostat and reflective dome add 2 inches of height.

There is one accessory to the Outback Oven that is a necessity. It's a pair of potgrabs, or hot-pot tongs. Potgrabs consist of right-angle clamps that you can use to pick up a pot that doesn't have a handle. The thermostat serves as a handle for the lid.

At first glance, it might look like the Outback Oven could slide off the burner if the boat rolls, which would be a risk if in a seaway or if the boat rolled violently. But the base plate and the aluminum frying pan are surprisingly skid resistant and the center of gravity is low, so the oven should be as safe to use in a reasonably quiet anchorage as any pot. If your stove is gimballed and/or has sea rails and pot clamps that fasten to the sea rails, there's an even greater safety factor.

But even without sea rails and pot clamps, you should be able to steady the oven by gripping it briefly with the fiberglass dome if a rude boater comes through the anchorage throwing a big wake. The outside of the dome should not be hot enough to burn your hands.

An alternative to the Outback Oven that works well as a stovetop oven is one with which you've probably had some practice: a pressure cooker. Yes, a pressure cooker—but without the pressure.

You can convert your conventional pressure cooker into an oven by removing both the rubber gasket and the rubber safety valve from the lid. Then place the baking pan on the metal rack in the bottom of the pressure cooker. Then lock the lid in place (it will be a loose fit without the gasket) and put the cooker on the burner. Bread can be baked by putting the dough directly into the cooker without the rack, but the bottom and sides of the pressure cooker should be oiled and coated liberally with either oatmeal or cornmeal on the bottom and sides as an insulating layer to keep the bread from scorching.

In practice, most people use the pressure cooker "oven" with a flame tamer (see opposite), starting with a fairly high heat for the first 10 minutes or so, then reducing the flame to a low-to-moderate level and letting things bake for another 20 minutes before cracking the lid to see how the dish is doing. If you find there is too much heat escaping through the hole in the lid created by removing the rubber safety valve, a wood plug in the hole will take care of that.

In any case, you'll need to be patient. The food in a pressure-cooker oven bakes mostly from the bottom up (the lid likely will never get too hot for you to touch). As a result, it takes longer for food to bake than in your oven at home or even in the Outback Oven. Trying to hurry it by turning up the flame will result in burning the bottom of your dinner. Coating the bottom of your baking dish with oil and cornmeal or oatmeal, as suggested previously for baking bread, will also protect the bottom of your creation from scorching.

■ FLAME TAMER

Flame tamers are also called flame spreaders, heat diffusers, or simmering rings, but they all do the same thing. They spread the heat from a gas, alcohol, or kerosene burner evenly across the bottom of your frying pan or pot, thereby eliminating the problem of hot spots. This process helps prevent scorching.

Depending on the age and features on your stove, a flame tamer can also fill an important safety function on a boat. Because it is most often used when you are cooking over low heat, the flame tamer lets you keep a flame on the burner that is strong enough so you don't have to worry about an errant breeze blowing out the flame and allowing your pressurized fuel to escape into the boat's cabin.

We've seen two designs. The one we prefer is inexpensive (generally about $5) and is sold in the kitchen sections of some discount stores and at many hardware stores. If you have trouble finding one, your nearest Ace hardware store can order one for you; just ask for the "simmering ring/heat diffuser," part number 331-777. Or go to www.acehardware.com and search for "simmer plate."

Our flame tamer consists of two metal skins held about $1/4$ inch apart and peppered with hundreds of small holes. It's round, about 9 inches in diameter, and has a wooden handle so that you can pick it up when it's hot.

More than twelve years old, Sea Sparrow's *well-used flame tamer is still going strong.*

To use a flame tamer, place it on the burner after lighting the flame, and put the pan, pot, or pressure-cooker oven on it. It's perfect for cooking something like rice, which needs a low heat to cook away the water without scorching the rice—difficult at best with a gas burner. Using a flame tamer means you need a slightly higher flame, and yes, a little more fuel consumption, but it's worth it.

COOKING UTENSILS

■ POTS AND PANS

In an ideal world, you'd have room for two frying pans. One would be a relatively small (10 inches) sauté pan with a nonstick or anodized surface. Preferably, it should be a heavyweight, thick-bottom pan, such as Calphalon, to help distribute the heat evenly and prevent the hot spots that typically form when cooking with a flame. You shouldn't need to use your flame tamer for everything! This frying pan is ideally suited for cooking eggs and other foods that you want to slide out of the pan in one piece.

The second frying pan would be up to 12 inches in diameter and have relatively high, straight sides. It would have a nonstick surface and a thick bottom, too, but a stainless steel pan with a thick-clad bottom also would work well. If it has a lid, all the better. This pan would be well suited to frying foods and to preparing larger meals. If, however, you don't have space to carry this second frying pan, you can use a 2-quart pot in its place.

Speaking of going to pot(s), although a 1-quart pot will do for most of the recipes here, a 2-quart pot gives you more flexibility. Again, we suggest a thick bottom and a nonstick surface or stainless steel.

■ PRESSURE COOKERS

If you've got the space, a pressure cooker is a great seagoing pot, whether or not you want it for a stovetop oven. It's a pot that some of us haven't seen used since our mothers or grandmothers were cooking for us, but many cruisers have found them to be very useful additions to their galley. Plus, there's

To rig Sea Sparrow's *pressure cooker as a stovetop oven, we removed the rubber gasket and safety valve and the weight from the lid. The flame tamer helps prevent hot spots.*

nothing better for cooking dried beans (don't forget the garlic!).

If you don't already have a pressure cooker, take a ruler or tape measure along when you go shopping. We suggest looking for one with an inside diameter of 10 inches—big enough for a 9-inch cake pan to fit loosely (make sure your cake pan doesn't have "handles" that add an inch or so to its size!). At the least, you'll want it to fit an 8-inch cake pan comfortably.

Your new pressure cooker will come with an instruction book, which you should read and carry with you. Along with instructions for using your pressure cooker safely and tables of suggested cooking times for different foods, it will have a number of recipes you can try.

The cooking times provided in the manual for John and Susan's Presto pressure cooker (plus a few additions) are shown in the tables (see pages 14–19) and can be used as guides, but they may differ slightly from the recommendations for your cooker. You can use these tables to estimate pressure-cooking times for many of the recipes in the Pot chapter. The fresh vegetable table gives you time guidelines according to size. In general, soups will cook in about 15 minutes (start timing when the pressure regulator begins to rock), with added time for the cooldown. Stews made with bite-size pieces of meat, potatoes, etc., will take about 6 to 7 minutes if you let the cooker cool down by itself, or 8 minutes if you depressurize it immediately. Note that the time it takes the pressure cooker to come to pressure will differ according the type and quantity of food you're cooking, but once it's at pressure—the regulator is rocking—the cooking time will be the same. See the cooking timetables below for more information.

The pressure-cooker recipes (see pages 121–25) in this book suggest allowing the cooker to depressurize itself by setting it aside for a few minutes and waiting for the pressure-relief valve to click down rather than by running cold water over the top (which is the standard way to depressurize it).

There are two reasons for this suggestion. First, you avoid wasting precious potable water when depressurizing the cooker. Second, the cooking time is about 20 percent shorter if you let it depressurize itself. The shorter cooking time conserves stove fuel and reduces the stove heat added to the cabin in hot weather. So if you use this system and are following someone else's recipe or the cooking timetables below, don't forget to adjust down the cooking times accordingly, if the times given assume you'll depressurize the cooker immediately. If you prefer to depressurize the cooker at once and are cruising in an area with clean (unpolluted) water, fresh or salt, you can use seawater to depressurize the cooker.

POULTRY TIMETABLE

Do not allow any of the poultry to reach above the cooker's $^2/_3$-full mark.

Poultry	Liquid (cups)	Cooking Time (minutes)
2$^1/_2$–3-pound whole chicken	1$^1/_2$	10–12
chicken, cut into serving pieces	1$^1/_2$	8
boneless chicken breast	1$^1/_2$	3–5*
3–4-pound turkey breast	2	35
Cornish hen	1$^1/_2$	8

*Depressurize the cooker immediately to prevent overcooking.

Adapted from Presto pressure cooker instruction manual, National Presto Industries.

SEAFOOD TIMETABLE

Use 1 cup of water in the cooker with seafood on rack. Do not fill the cooker more than $2/3$ full. Cook with the regulator rocking gently. To prevent overcooking, depressurize the cooker at once by running cold water over it or by placing it in the sink or a large pan with 1 to 2 inches of cold water.

Seafood	Cooking Time, fresh or thawed (minutes)	Cooking Time, frozen (minutes)
crab legs	2	2
fish fillets, 1 inch thick	2	2
lobster tail, 6 to 8 ounces	5	10–12
lobster tail, 12 to 14 ounces	8	12–13
salmon steaks, $1/2$ inch thick	2	2
scallops, small	1	1
scallops, medium or large	2	2
shrimp, small	1	1
shrimp, medium	2	2
shrimp, large	3	3

Adapted from Presto pressure cooker instruction manual, National Presto Industries.

MEAT TIMETABLE

Do not allow any of the meat to reach above the cooker's $2/3$-full mark.

Meat	Liquid (cups)	Cooking Time (minutes)
Beef		
chuck roast, $1^1/2$ pounds	$1^1/2$	25
chuck roast, 3 pounds	$1^1/2$	35
corned beef, 3 pounds	2	60
rolled rib roast, 3 pounds	$1^1/2$	30
round steak, $1/4$ inch thick	1	4*
round steak, $1/2$ inch thick	1	10*
short ribs	2	25*

Meat	Liquid (cups)	Cooking Time (minutes)
Ham		
slice, 3 pounds	1½	30
picnic, 3 pounds	1½	30
Lamb		
chops, ¼ inch thick	½	2*
chops, ½ inch thick	½	5*
leg, 3 pounds	1½	35–45
Pork		
chops, ¼ inch thick	1	2*
chops, ½ inch thick	1	5*
butt roast, 3 pounds	3	55
loin roast, 3 pounds	3	60
steak, ¼ inch thick	½	2*
steak, ½ inch thick	½	5*
Veal		
chops, ¼ inch thick	½	2*
chops, ½ inch thick	½	5*
roast, 3 pounds	2	45
steak, 1 inch thick	1	10*

*Depressurize the cooker at once to prevent overcooking.

Adapted from Presto pressure cooker instruction manual, National Presto Industries.

FRESH VEGETABLE TIMETABLE

For crunchy vegetables, cook the minimum time shown; for soft vegetables, cook the maximum time. To prevent overcooking, depressurize cooker at once. If cooking time is 0 minutes, stop cooking as soon as the regulator begins to rock.

Vegetable	Size	Liquid (cups)	Cooking Time (minutes)
artichoke (wash, trim, and score hearts)	whole	1	10

Vegetable	Size	Liquid (cups)	Cooking Time (minutes)
asparagus	tips	$1/2$	0–1
asparagus	stems (1-inch pieces)	$1/2$	0–2
beans, green or wax	whole or pieces	$1/2$	1–3
beans, lima (wash and shell)	whole	$1/2$	1–2
beets (wash thoroughly; remove all but 2 inches of tops; leave roots on; skins slip off after cooking)	whole ($2\frac{1}{2}$-inch diameter)	$1\frac{1}{2}$	15
broccoli	whole (1-inch diameter stem)	$1/2$	1–2
brussels sprouts	whole (1-inch diameter)	$1/2$	1–3
cabbage	wedge (2 inches)	$1/2$	1–3
cabbage	wedge ($3\frac{1}{2}$ inches)	1	1–5
carrots	whole ($1\frac{1}{4}$-inch diameter)	1	4–8
carrots	slices ($1/4$ inch thick)	$1/2$	1–2
cauliflower	florets	$1/2$	0–2
cauliflower	whole (6-inch diameter)	1	2–5
celery	whole or pieces	$1/2$	0–2
corn on the cob, shucked	whole ($2\frac{1}{2}$-inch diameter)	$1/2$	2–3
greens (beet, spinach, Swiss chard, turnip)	whole leaves	$1/2$	0–3
kohlrabi	cubes or slices (1 inch thick)	1	3
onions	whole (2-inch diameter)	1	5

FRESH VEGETABLE TIMETABLE (cont.)

Vegetable	Size	Liquid (cups)	Cooking Time (minutes)
parsnips	slices ($1/4$ inch thick)	$1/2$	0–2
parsnips	whole (2-inch diameter)	1	10
peas, green (shelled)	whole	$1/2$	0–2
potatoes	slices ($1/2$ inch thick)	$1/2$	3
potatoes	slices ($3/4$ inch thick)	1	5
potatoes	whole ($1^1/2$-inch diameter)	1	10
potatoes	whole ($2^1/2$-inch diameter)	$1^1/2$	15
pumpkin	wedges (2 by 3 inches)	1	10
rutabaga	cubes or slices (1 inch thick)	$1/2$	3
squash, summer	slices ($1/2$ inch thick)	$1/2$	35 seconds and slow cooldown
squash, winter	cubes or slices (1 inch thick)	$1^1/2$	12
sweet potatoes (cut large ones in half or cook 15 minutes)	whole	1	10
turnips	cubes or slices (1 inch thick)	$1/2$	3

Adapted from Presto pressure cooker instruction manual, National Presto Industries.

DRIED VEGETABLE TIMETABLE

To prepare beans for cooking, soak them overnight in the cooker (they will expand when soaked, so use plenty of water) with 1 tablespoon of salt and $1/4$ cup of cooking oil. We recommend an additional soaking round, which reduces problems with intestinal discomfort. So in the morning, drain the beans, add fresh soaking water, and soak all day. For cooking, drain the soaking water and add enough fresh water to more than cover the beans. Do not fill the cooker more than half full. With the times provided, allow the cooker to depressurize itself.

Warning: Pressure-cook only the dried vegetables listed below. Do not pressure-cook split peas, pearl barley, or soup mixes containing dried vegetables as they can clog the vent pipe.

Vegetable	Cooking Time (minutes)
black beans	35
black-eyed peas	20
great northern beans	30
green peas, whole	5
kidney beans	25
lentils	20
lima beans	25
navy beans	30
pink beans	30
pinto beans	25
yellow peas, whole	5

Adapted from Presto pressure cooker instruction manual, National Presto Industries.

■ OTHER USEFUL GALLEY GEAR

If you have a pressure cooker, a vital accessory is a set of stainless steel mixing bowls, most of which will fit inside the cooker. The bowls will be worth whatever space they take.

For example, you can cook rice in your pressure cooker if you use a stainless steel mixing bowl. You can even get fancy and cook meat with your rice. But you've got to have that mixing bowl to do it. Those same mixing bowls will also make excellent baking dishes if you use the pressure cooker for a stovetop oven. A set of potgrabs, such as those used with the Outback Oven, is also handy for lifting baking pans/bowls out of a hot pressure cooker.

A wooden cutting board is another vital piece of galley equipment. Not only will you need it to cut all those fresh veggies you'll use when creating your mouthwatering meals, but it can also do double duty as a hot pad to protect your countertop and table. But remember, a wooden cutting board can present food safety issues such as cross-contamination or even toxic possibilities if you neglect to clean and sanitize the board thoroughly after use. So also invest in some inexpensive cutting mats; they're made of flexible plastic for easy cleanup, they're easy to stow, and they're color-coded so that you don't use the seafood mat (blue) to prepare veggies (green).

Finally, if you like fried food (see the wonderful recipes for fried foods on pages 56–60), a boat's galley can really benefit from a spatter screen. These screens are readily available wherever kitchen utensils are sold, and you'll need one for the larger frying pan. Your boat's galley is too compact and too intimately involved with the rest of your living quarters to have grease spattering the surroundings.

REFRIGERATORS, ICEBOXES, AND COOLERS

Cruisers lucky enough to have a refrigerator in their galley have an advantage when cruising in remote areas, but iceboxes and coolers can provide all the "refrigeration" you need for several days at a time if they are well insulated and you use them sensibly. If your boat does not have either a built-in refrigerator or an icebox, you can fill the gap quite nicely with portable coolers and/or a portable 12-volt refrigerator-freezer.

First, let's look at the advantages and disadvantages of refrigeration. On the plus side, you have the ease and convenience of a refrigerator and freezer. That's something that can't be minimized. On the negative side, a refrigerator, whether built-in or portable, is an energy hog. Although energy requirements will vary with the outside temperature and the efficiency of your unit's insulation, cruisers typically must run their engines about two hours (give or take half an hour) every morning and night just to keep the fridge cold. If you'll be motoring that much anyway, there's no problem. If, however, you're staying in an anchorage for a few days or mostly sailing, you still have to run your engine (or generator) to power the refrigerator.

If you have an icebox, you don't have to worry about energy, but you also don't really have a refrigerator or a freezer. All you have is an icebox. And let's face it, ice melts.

A well-insulated icebox filled halfway or more with ice will keep its cool for a week or longer; more in colder weather, a little less in the tropics. As a result, you must either plan your itinerary to replenish the ice supply or do without ice after the box warms up. So you can't be as carefree as you might be with a refrigerator.

Coolers obviously won't do as well, but even they will keep ice for a long weekend if you don't open them too often. Moreover, if you combine your cooler with a portable freezer that runs on 12 volts, you may be able to keep the cooler going indefinitely.

One such unit we've seen is the Engel 14-quart capacity portable freezer. It's actually a miniature refrigerator or freezer (as opposed to a "thermoelectric cooler") that draws 1 amp per hour in the refrigerator mode and 3.9 amps in the freezer mode and operates between 0 and 44°F. We know of cruisers who have used one of these units to freeze blue ice packets for use in their cooler, rotating them about every twelve hours. The system works if you're motoring a lot or charging your batteries morning and night, but you've got to watch the power consumption. In addition, this refrigerator should have its own large-capacity, deep-cycle battery.

Finally, if you're thinking about cruising with an icebox or cooler and are concerned about the cost of ice, consider this. Our experience suggests that the operating costs for an icebox versus a refrigerator are at worst an even trade-off. Buying ice may seem more expensive than running a refrigerator but it's not. When John and Susan compared *Sea Sparrow*'s ice costs over a two-year period to the cost of burning a couple of gallons of diesel fuel every day to keep a fridge cold, the cost of ice was about half the cost of the diesel, even with the high cost of ice in some island areas. And that doesn't take into consideration either the initial cost of refrigeration or wear and tear on the engine.

■ TIPS FOR KEEPING YOUR COOL

If you've got a refrigerator, one of the most useful accessories you can install is a small circulating fan, like the Valterra Fridgemate 3-volt fan (www.valterra.com), which evens out the temperature in the box. The Fridgemate will run for a month on two D-cell batteries.

There are also little tricks you can use to help keep your cool. Some apply only to iceboxes or coolers, but others are also useful for refrigerators. Some are just common sense, such as keeping your cooler or portable fridge out of the sun and away from the engine. (In other words, if you'll be using the engine, a cockpit locker next or open to the engine room is not a good place!) Another is opening the icebox, cooler, or fridge only when necessary. If you want cold drinks, keep them in a separate cooler.

Here are some other tips we have collected from cruisers over the years.

- *Line your fridge, icebox, or cooler with a space blanket. It will tend to reflect heat to the outside and cold to the inside.*

- *Leave home with all but your first day's meat frozen hard (freeze for at least two days).*

- *Build an ice nest for your frozen food so there is ice below the food, on all four sides, and on top. The idea is to make your frozen food a core part of the ice in the box. This is a good idea in your refrigerator, too. Putting a load of ice in the bottom enables it to operate much more efficiently, which cuts down on the engine time needed to keep the fridge cold.*

- *Cover the ice with another space blanket. If you have other items (not drinks) that you want to keep chilled, place them on top of the space blanket, if there's still room, or keep them in a different cooler. Fill your icebox or cooler to the brim, using scrunched-up plastic trash bags if necessary to fill the space, and then top it all off with another space blanket.*

   The idea is to keep air spaces in the icebox to a minimum. And as you take things out of the box, or as the ice melts, keep adding fillers (e.g., more scrunched-up plastic trash bags) to take up the space. It will make the ice last longer.

- *Finally, wrap a piece of closed-cell foam in a terry cloth towel and keep it on top of your icebox or cooler. You'll be surprised by how much added insulation it provides. Even a beach towel or two folded in several layers and draped over the icebox or cooler will provide extra insulation, making your ice last longer.*

You may have to experiment a little to find out how long you can keep your icebox or cooler cold, but you'll probably find that it's longer than you think (ice in *Sea Sparrow*'s icebox lasts up to ten days). After you've got it figured out, you can plan your menu and trips ashore to the store accordingly.

Some of the foods we routinely keep in the refrigerator at home don't really need refrigeration. Butter and margarine are examples. If it's too hot, butter will melt, of course, as will tub margarine. Want to cut down on trans-fatty acids? There are some healthy margarines, and consider packing some extra-virgin olive oil instead if you need to lube up your toast in the morning. Ketchup, mustard, jams, syrup, pickles, molasses, and honey don't need refrigeration. Nor do vacuum-packed hard cheeses, individually wrapped slices of cheese, or a Gouda cheese in red wax. On the meat side, pepperoni, summer sausage, and salami will keep for three or four days after opening without refrigeration, even in the tropics. And there are canned meats and softpack products like Tyson's chicken breast meat and tuna that can survive without chilling until they're opened. Stowing these items in lockers instead of the icebox or cooler leaves more room for ice.

KITCHEN SOFTWARE

Galleys, like computers, need "software" to function well. And in the galley, your software consists of seasonings, spices, and oils. Depending on your boat's size, you can stock the galley with spices that come directly from the grocery store. If space is at a premium, however, use any small plastic vials or other unbreakable containers to store spices, taking only what the menu calls for on each cruise.

Clear plastic film containers and empty prescription pill bottles will also keep spices fresh. (You can get empty film canisters from your local express photo-processing lab. Ask your pharmacist for large pill bottles.) Label these containers clearly. An excellent alternative to pill bottles or film canisters is a seven-day pillbox—get the large size. Label each compartment with white adhesive tape.

Spices and seasonings suggested as a minimum include the following:

salt	Cajun spices	Parmesan cheese
pepper	basil	bouillon cubes
seasoned salt	thyme	sugar
onion flakes	marjoram	
garlic powder	bay leaves	
celery salt	paprika	
hot sauce/Tabasco	oregano	

Your galley software should also include a variety of oils. Vegetable, olive, peanut, canola, and/or corn oils (packed as needed for recipes selected) in 4-ounce bottles should suffice for most short cruises. You can also buy several of the 8-ounce bottles of olive oil, pour the oil from three or four of these bottles into a large container for use at home, and relabel the empty 8-ounce bottles for use with your other oils. Whatever you do, be sure to pack the oils so that the bottles remain upright. It's also a good idea to wrap each bottle with paper towels, both as cushioning and to keep the bottles "dry."

Now, on to the food!

the
Food

We've talked about your galley's hardware and software, so now let's look at planning your gastronomic pleasures afloat while still in the comfort of your living room.

HOW TO PLAN A MENU

Your body is an engine powered by the food (i.e., the calories) that you eat. Even in warm weather, you can require up to 4,000 calories per day when you're out on the water, particularly if you're racing or in an active weather system. In colder conditions, you can use up even more calories trying to keep warm as the wind chill penetrates your foul-weather gear. So, although you can plan any meals you like, you have to build plenty of high-quality calories into them. And remember that these calories must be derived from the right sources.

Although most of the recipes here represent a balanced diet of meat and vegetable protein, there's nothing about vegetarianism that is incompatible with boating or any other physical activity. For example, Don's backpacking friend Chris Townsend is a vegetarian, has many 1,000-mile-plus hikes under his belt, and has done them all on vegetables! So there's no reason why boaters can't survive the rigors of our waterways and oceans on vegetarian meals as well. And fortunately for our palates, Chris contributed a couple of his favorite recipes to this book. Whatever your preference, plan your meals to include ample quantities of the four major food groups over the course of a day.

Dairy. Dairy products include milk, cheese, pudding, yogurt, and tofu.

Meat. Meats include beef, pork, poultry, fish, and shellfish; vegetarian options include dried beans, peanut butter, eggs, nuts, and seeds.

Vegetables and fruits. All fruits, all vegetables; green and leafy veggies are excellent sources of roughage. Self-packaged and easy-cooking choices include summer squash and green peppers.

Grains. Grains include cereal, noodles, pasta, rice, grits, breads, and popcorn.

You'll notice that most portions in this book are pretty large. At home, for example, the average size for meat portions should be 3 to 4 ounces, but on the water—unless you're just lazing in the cockpit—you'll need more.

Using these recipes, figure an average dinner serving to be about 4-plus ounces of meat (note that the softpack chicken we mention usually comes in 7-ounce packages); $3/4$ cup of vegetables (rehydrated if you're using dried peas, beans, etc.); about 2 to 3 ounces of bread or $1/2$ cup of noodles or rice; and a full piece of fruit (if fresh) or $1/2$ cup of dried fruits such as apricots, raisins, and prunes. Although the meat portion is slightly elevated relative to an inactive diet, and the carbohydrate intake is increased, the fats are few. Ideally, you should look at holding your fat calories to 30 percent of your daily intake, with another 20 to 30 percent devoted to protein. The balance is filled in by faster-burning carbs. Your needs and desires may vary. Nutritional substitutes are fine. See the following for some meat alternatives.

■ MEAT SUBSTITUTES

To obtain the equivalent level of protein found in 1 ounce of meat, substitute as follows:

> **1 egg**
> $1/4$ **cup cashews, walnuts, almonds, pecans, or sunflower seeds**
> $1^1/2$ **cups cooked oatmeal**
> **1 ounce cheese**
> **2 tablespoons peanut butter**
> $1/2$ **cup whole wheat flour**

To go farther—and to ensure that you get all nine amino acids essential for your body's protein synthesis—practice protein complementation. Here's how this works: The food combinations listed in the following table take advantage of protein complementation to provide a complete protein. Each item on the list contains all essential amino acids needed for protein synthesis.

Dairy Products or Eggs with Grains

bread or rice pudding

cereal and milk

cheese fondue with bread

cheese sandwich

creamed soups with noodles
    or rice

eggs and toast

egg salad sandwich

fettucine (pasta and cheese)

French toast

macaroni and cheese

meatless lasagna

pancakes or waffles

pizza

quiche

yogurt and crackers

Grains with Legumes

baked beans and brown bread

bean or lentil soup and bread

bean and rice dishes

corn tortillas or tacos and beans

hummus and bread

lentils and rice

peanut butter sandwich

soybean sandwich

split pea soup and cornbread

tamale pie (beans and cornmeal)

quinoa (a complete protein package
    by itself)

Nuts and Seeds with Legumes

bean soup with sesame seed muffins

hummus with sesame seeds

nuts and seed snacks

roasted soybeans and seed snacks

tofu with sesame seeds

Other Vegetables with Dairy Products or Eggs

bean-cheese salad

cream of vegetable soup

eggplant-artichoke Parmesan

scalloped potatoes

potato salad with egg

spinach or broccoli quiche

spinach salad with eggs and cheese

The bottom line is this: No one-pan menu is complete unless you obtain the nourishment you need. Plan smart. Eat balanced meals. And don't skimp on the food you pack.

■ POWER BUYING

Because you'll be feeding yourself, the single most important guest at your floating table, don't cut corners on the quality of the food you purchase. Fresh is always best, but there are times to use tinned or soft-packaged meats, dried fruits and vegetables, or other prepared foods to facilitate your efforts. Just remember that whatever you carry onto your boat, you also have to take off the boat when you get to a marina or boat ramp. That means cans, wrappers, foils, and the like. Avoid recipes that demand out-of-season vegetables or other exotic items.

As for meats, you might consider making friends with a good butcher. They tend to carry slightly better, though more expensive, cuts of meat, and you're better assured that the meat is fresh, not previously frozen.

For the most part, vegetables and fruits should always be ripe but firm. One notable exception is bananas. We like to get a progression of ripeness for bananas (from very green to ready to eat) so that we have bananas ripening every day instead of having them all ripen at the same time.

Powdered milk is an acceptable substitute for fresh when mixed in a ratio of 1 part powder to 3 parts water. However, mixing an entire packet of powder (designed to make 1 quart of milk) with just 1 to 2 cups of water, depending on how thick you want the end result, works fine in the recipes, and leftovers taste great in coffee. Unless you're depending on the milk fat for use in a sauce (evaporated milk may be the only solution in that case), powdered milk cooks well.

Cheese, however, is the greatest invention to make sure you get enough milk protein and fat. Moreover, it keeps well and doesn't take up much space.

The "when" in shopping is just as important as the "what." Meats should be bought at least two days in advance to allow for freezing (see next section). Fruits and veggies can wait until the day before or, even better, the morning you leave. Most food stores restock throughout the day, but tend to get their shipments early. The first fruits and vegetables on display are probably fresher than the ones that show up later in the day.

GETTING THE SHOW READY FOR THE ROAD

Creativity plays a big role when you're packing in a confined space. Repackaging, with a concentration on maintaining freshness and avoiding food poisoning, is a priority.

For a long weekend, for example, we suggest you begin by planning your menus to determine what cuts of meat you'll need and in what weights. By wrapping each meal's meat portion in heavy-duty, freezer-thickness aluminum foil and parking the package in the deep freeze for two days, you'll have them well frozen for your cruise. Then, about 10 minutes before loading everything into the trunk of your car to go to the boat, pull the meat out of the freezer and wrap it in another layer of foil—loosely this time to leave some air space. Then drop it into the cooler with its ice packs. After you're on the boat, you can transfer the meat into your refrigerator or icebox, or stow the cooler where it's out of the sun. In this way, the meat will stay frozen for almost as long as there is ice. The hard frozen meat also helps to keep other items in the cooler, icebox, or refrigerator cold.

■ PACKAGING IDEAS

If you look for them, you'll find an incredible number of condiments packed in single-serving packets. Items such as soy sauce, ketchup, mustard, honey, syrup, and mayonnaise are packed so that they require no refrigeration and little space. Find these condiments (even if you have to use leftovers from your local fast-food emporium) and pack them away.

Other items demand more creative solutions. Oils can be remeasured into vials, squeeze bottles, or even baby bottles. Flour, baking powder, pancake mix, and other dry ingredients can be measured into plastic bags and sealed. Remember to label them!

For long-term storage, consider getting an inexpensive vacuum-packing system. Use this system to vacuum-pack dry ingredients in heavy-duty, heat-sealed plastic bags. To keep weevils from your dry goods, put a bay leaf in each package.

Vegetables often come in their own wrappers. (Have you ever seriously contemplated an onion?) So do some fruits. That's what makes fresh food so easy to handle.

Although eggs may require some cushioning to absorb shock and need to be turned over weekly if you're trying to keep them for a long time, the bigger problem is to avoid crushing them. *Sea Sparrow*'s hard plastic egg carton has kept eggs secure under all kinds of sea conditions and makes it easy to turn them over.

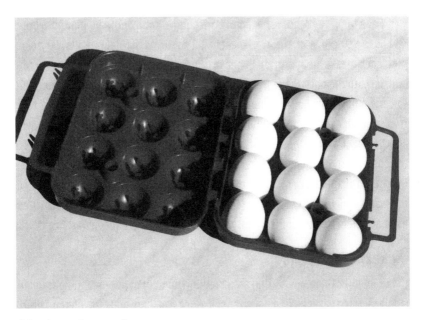

A hard carrying case for eggs.

A short length of shock cord wrapped around the container provides insurance against the carton coming open accidentally.

For a short cruise or for the first few days of a longer cruise, rice and pasta can be cooked at home, packaged in a plastic bag (this cuts down on time and work in the galley), and stored in a cooler. A light touch of oil mixed into the pasta or rice immediately after taking it off the stove will keep it from turning into a clump.

Again, most of these tips come under the heading of common sense.

THE ONE-PAN MENU

The most common denominator for a cruise length is two days—i.e., a weekend. Assuming that you leave after dinner Friday and plan to be back at the marina or boat ramp sometime Sunday afternoon, it means planning for five meals. The five standard repasts are Saturday breakfast, lunch, and dinner; and Sunday breakfast and lunch. You might also consider a late snack or dinner on Friday night.

In general, it's worthwhile being pretty generous with yourself when planning your food. You never can tell when you might need an extra portion for a visitor. Or maybe that "Sunday morning return home" turns into a "Sunday evening, I'm late thanks to the weather." That extra meal can come in handy.

Before moving on to some sample weekend menus, here's a suggestion for a lunch that tastes great and provides plenty of calories to keep you going until dinner. Don picked up this updated version of historic voyageur fare as an adult leader on a Boy Scout Canoeing High Adventure in Minnesota's Boundary Waters some years ago, and it kept a group of teenage boys going. It was lunch for five of the nine days they were out. (Lunch the other days included beef stick, cheese, and hard crackers.) The recipe is not included elsewhere because you can make it ahead of time and use it either for one of your planned meals or as backup.

Prepare this at home. Cut and wrap as many pieces as you need for your cruise. Then add a few more for a reserve.

Hudson Bay Bread

$3/4$ cup ($1^1/2$ sticks) butter or margarine
1 cup sugar
3 tablespoons Karo syrup
3 tablespoons honey
$1/2$ teaspoon maple flavoring
$1/3$ cup ground nuts (any combination)
4 cups uncooked old-fashioned oatmeal

Cream together the first five ingredients. Combine the nuts and oatmeal and then mix with the creamed mixture. Spread in a preheated and greased 9-by-9-by-2-inch baking pan. (Press mixture down to a thickness of about $1^1/2$ inches.) Bake at 325°F for 25 minutes (check at about 20 minutes to prevent burning). When bread is done, remove from oven and immediately press down firmly with spatula. Cut into serving sizes (about the same as a slice of bread) while still warm. Makes 6 servings.

Serve this bread topped with peanut butter and jelly. You'll have a cold lunch that tastes great and is very filling. One slice should do it. You can substitute Hudson Bay Bread for any lunch you want.

■ SAMPLE WEEKEND MENUS

When you plan your cruise menu, the first step is to decide whether you feel like eating pan, pot, or oven food—or some combination thereof. Here are three possible menus and associated shopping lists for a modest weekend outing, reaching the boat after dinner on Friday and heading home after Sunday breakfast or lunch. Build from there for longer cruises. (See the appendix for a sample week-long menu.)

The first menu includes a cooked lunch and requires only a frying pan.

Saturday Breakfast

sliced oranges

Vegetable Eggs (see page 39)

Saturday Lunch

Parmy Shrooms 'n' Noodles (see page 64)

pear, apple, or melon slices

Saturday Dinner

sliced tomato

Hair-Raisin Curry Beef or Chicken Scallopine (see pages 73 and 50)

rice

Coconuts to You Fruit Cup (see page 78)

Sunday Breakfast

ham slice

Apple Pancakes or Huevos and Tacos (see pages 45 and 41)

Sunday Lunch

Hudson Bay Bread (see page 31)

peanut butter

jelly

Repackage the meat, cheeses, milk, and flour. Precook the noodles and spaghetti and repackage. You can also take along various snacks and hot drinks (coffee, hot chocolate, V-8 Juice). The key is to get plenty of calories to keep up your energy, which, incidentally, preserves your body core temperature so you don't get chilled as easily.

SHOPPING LIST

Provisions (staples)	Carbs	Proteins	Vegetables/ Fruits	Fats/ Oils	Sweeteners/ Spices
coffee	rice (small pkg.)	peanut butter (small)	oranges	nuts (¹/₃ cup)	jelly (small)
juice mix	potatoes (2 med.)	eggs (11)	pears	peanuts (¹/₃ cup unsalted)	coconut (¹/₄ cup)
milk (powdered)	tortillas (4)	ham (¹/₂ cup diced, 1 slice)	apples	black olives (2 tbsp.)	Karo syrup (3 tbsp.)
hot chocolate mix	bread- crumbs (small pkg.)	sirloin (³/₄ lb.)	bananas	peanut oil (1 tbsp.)	honey (3 tbsp.)
wine	oatmeal (4 cups uncooked)	chicken breasts (2)	melon	olive oil (3 tbsp.)	maple flavoring (¹/₂ tsp.)
flour			raisins (¹/₂ cup)		
nonstick cooking spray	noodles (1¹/₂ cups)	cheese (¹/₄ lb. Muenster, ¹/₃ cup diced other, ¹/₄ cup Parmesan)	tomatoes	butter or margarine (1 cup)	maple syrup (¹/₂ cup)
salt	spaghetti or other pasta (2 cups)		green peppers (2)	shortening (1 tbsp.)	chicken and beef bouil- lon cubes (1 ea.)
pepper (black and white)	Bisquick (³/₄ cup)		onions (3)		Tabasco sauce (dash)
sugar (white, brown, sugar subst.)			mushrooms (9)		curry powder (¹/₂ tbsp.)
			avocado (1)		cinnamon (¹/₂ tsp.)
			garlic (1 clove)		nutmeg (¹/₂ tsp.)

Here's a weekend menu using a pot.

Saturday Breakfast

Eggs à la Goldenrod (see page 86)

Saturday Lunch

Fast Pea Soup (see page 99)

Saturday Dinner

Pedro's Rice (see page 112)

Indian Pudding (see page 125)

Snacks

oranges

Sunday Breakfast

Soy Sauce Steak Sunrise (see page 84)

hard-boiled eggs

SHOPPING LIST

Provisions (staples)	Carbs	Proteins	Vegetables/ Fruits	Fats/Oils	Sweeteners/ Spices
coffee	bread (4 slices)	eggs (6+)	oranges	butter or margarine (3 tbsp.)	thyme (1 tsp.)
juice mix	rice (3/4 cup uncooked)	ham (1/2 cup diced)	tomatoes (5 plum)		chili powder (1/2 tsp.)
milk (powdered)	cornmeal (3/4 cup)	ground beef (1/2 lb.)	raisins (1/4 cup)		nutmeg (1/2 tsp.)
hot chocolate mix	crackers	sirloin (1/2 lb.)	peas (1 cup freeze-dried)		cinnamon (1/2 tsp.)
wine			onion (1)		soy sauce (1/3 cup)
flour			green pepper (1)		honey (2 tbsp.)
nonstick cooking spray			carrots (2)		sweetened condensed milk (1 can)
salt					
pepper (black and white)					
sugar (white, brown, sugar subst.)					

Remember to repackage meat, milk powder, cornmeal, flour, and bread. Finally, here's a weekend menu using an oven.

Saturday Breakfast

Amsterdam Apple Pancake
(see page 133)

Saturday Lunch

beef stick

cheese

bread

carrots

Saturday Dinner

Cheesy Spuds (see page 147)

Blue-Tooth Cobbler (see page 169)

Snacks

cashews and raisins

Sunday Breakfast

Bermuda Eggs (see page 132)

SHOPPING LIST

Provisions (staples)	Carbs	Proteins	Vegetables/ Fruits	Fats/ Oils	Sweeteners/ Spices
coffee	bread	eggs (5)	apples (2)	cashews	nutmeg ($^1/_4$ tsp.)
juice mix	Bisquick ($1^2/_3$ cup)	beef stick ($^1/_3$ lb.)	blueberries ($^1/_2$ cup)	butter or margarine (4 tbsp.)	tarragon ($^1/_4$ tsp.)
milk (powdered)	potatoes (4)	ham (6 oz.)	raisins		cinnamon (1 tsp.)
hot chocolate mix	bread-crumbs (2 tbsp.)	cheese ($^1/_2$ cup cheddar, 1 tbsp. Parmesan, $^1/_2$ lb. other)	carrots		
wine			parsley (2 tbsp.)		
flour			onions (1 yellow, 1 Bermuda)		
nonstick cooking spray					
salt					
pepper (black and white)					
sugar (white, brown, sugar subst.)					

CLEANUP

One of the chores after any meal is washing the dishes and putting away the food. This is a time for the crew (and/or the captain) to show appreciation for the chef's work by pitching in to help with the cleanup. On some boats, in fact, the chef is excused completely from cleanup if the crew's duties permit. Whatever system you work out, make sure that the chef has a voice in it.

■ GARBAGE

That's food waste . . . soft stuff. You already know that you can't dump anything hard—bones, cans, jars, wrappers, six-pack carriers, etc.—overboard. But unless you're offshore, you also cannot—either in good conscience or legally—throw garbage overboard. You can minimize this issue by trimming your meat and vegetables before freezing or packaging them for the boat and/or by eating everything you've prepared—even if that means having some of it later as a snack. But you'll inevitably have some debris.

If you'll be away from an acceptable disposal area for several days, you can wrap anything that will ripen if left to its own devices in foil or plastic wrap and put it in your cooler, icebox, or fridge. Wrapping the garbage not only keeps it from getting smelly, but it also takes up some of the air space in your cooler. Moreover, the quantity should be small enough to not challenge the ice significantly.

But enough about the end of the meal. Let's start tantalizing your taste buds!

the
Frying Pan

So far, we've talked about the various pots, pans, kettles, ovens, and other para-phernalia you need to make sure your galley is up to your gastronomic ambitions. In this chapter, we'll get down to the brass tacks of eating. So, get a firm grip on your 12-inch frying pan (actually, size doesn't matter) and start cooking!

BREAKFAST

Most of us fondly remember the smell of thick-cut bacon sizzling in a pan, the crunch of toast as it's buttered, and the aroma of fresh-brewed coffee. Break-fast is the most important meal of the day. And breakfast out of a frying pan can be as simple as you want or elegantly challenging. Whatever . . . breakfast is the fuel that gives you the old get-up-and-go. So eat hearty and cruise on!

■ EGGS

They're fried, poached, and boiled. But scrambled is the baseline for eggers. It means never having to say you're sorry for broken yolks. You can spruce up scrambled eggs in any number of ways, with additions of meat, cheese, and/or spices. Here are some of our favorites.

☛ Note: All recipes make two servings unless otherwise indicated.

Spruced-Up Scrambled Eggs

5 large eggs

$^1/_4$ cup milk (fresh or powdered)

salt and pepper to taste

nonstick cooking spray

extras (see following list)

Beat eggs, milk, and salt and pepper in a bowl. Spray frying pan and heat over medium heat. Pour eggs into pan and let cook undisturbed for about 30 seconds. Add desired extras and mix in with spatula. Cook for 2 minutes, scraping bottom of pan as you continue to turn the eggs until dry (or as done as you like). Eat with a hard roll, fruit, and beverage.

EXTRAS

Meat	Cheese
diced ham or steak	diced block cheese
sliced hot dog, bologna, or salami	cubed cream cheese
chicken chunks	**Spices**
	Tabasco sauce
	oregano
	basil

If you're an egg fanatic, there are ways to make the dependable, edible egg more exciting. Try adding dried mushrooms, parsley, onions, or green peppers. For spice, add a few tablespoons of medium or hot salsa. Or put crunch into your meal with walnuts, cashews, or peanuts. And if you're really adventurous, try adding dried fruits, such as apricots, along with nuts.

Sometimes you have to make an even bigger meal out of breakfast. Spicing things up while getting something a bit more substantial into your stomach can make a damp and foggy morning on the water bright indeed.

Vegetable Eggs

nonstick cooking spray

2 medium potatoes, peeled and chopped ($3/4$ cup or so)

$1/2$ cup green pepper, chopped

1 small onion, chopped

salt and pepper to taste

4 eggs

$1/3$ cup diced cheese (optional)

2 tablespoons breadcrumbs (optional)

Spray frying pan and heat over medium heat. Sauté vegetables until browned but not crisp. Add salt and pepper to taste. Break eggs over vegetable mixture and cover pan. Lower heat and cook until eggs are to your liking. Sprinkle with cheese and breadcrumbs, if desired.

And if you want to be a bit more ethnic with your eggs, consider these three egg dishes. You'll think you're cruising around the Mediterranean when you taste them.

Eggs à la Haifa

> ¹/₄ pound kosher salami, sliced
> 1 teaspoon olive oil
> 5 eggs
> salt and pepper to taste
> 1 teaspoon peanut oil

Notch edges of salami slices so they won't curl while cooking. Preheat 10- or 12-inch frying pan, add olive oil, and cook salami slowly. Turn once so each side is crispy. Remove from heat and drain oil. In small bowl, beat eggs and season as desired with salt and pepper. Add peanut oil to pan. Return salami slices to pan and add eggs. Fry slowly, as for an omelet, until bottom is golden brown and top is firm. Slide out of pan onto plate and flip back into pan to brown top. Watch carefully to avoid burning.

———————

Flor-Egg-Enzo

> 1¹/₂ tablespoons olive oil
> 1 medium onion, diced
> pinch of salt
> ¹/₄ teaspoon pepper
> 1 large tomato, chopped
> 1 cup frozen peas, defrosted
> ¹/₂ cup water
> 4 eggs
> 3 tablespoons Parmesan cheese
> chunks of French or Italian bread (optional)

Preheat frying pan and add oil. Sauté onion until tender. Lower heat and add salt (if desired), pepper, and tomato. Simmer for about 10 minutes. Add peas and water; simmer another 10 minutes. Carefully break eggs into mixture in pan as you would for poached eggs. Continue cooking over low heat for another 15 minutes without stirring. Sprinkle with Parmesan. If desired, gently add chunks of bread to mixture about 10 minutes before serving to soak up a bit of sauce and thicken things.

☞ Tip: Serve by placing eggs on rounds of garlic toast and surrounding with vegetable sauce.

Huevos and Tacos

4 flour tortillas
4 eggs
1/4 pound Muenster cheese, chopped or grated
dash of Tabasco sauce
1 avocado, diced
2 tablespoons black olives, diced
nonstick cooking spray
salsa (optional)

Warm tortillas in dry frying pan; set aside in covered dish to keep warm. In a bowl, scramble eggs and mix in cheese and hot sauce. Spray pan and add scrambled egg and cheese mixture. When done, remove from heat and stir in avocado and olives. Spoon onto warm tortillas, roll, and top with salsa (if desired).

☞ Tip: Serve on plate garnished with orange slices.

You could say that omelets are scrambled eggs that have a sense of togetherness. You can customize your omelets any way you wish, but if you don't cook them right from the start, you might as well make scrambled eggs.

And the best way to make sure you are on the right track is to use the right pan. Although any frying pan can work, you will get the best results if you use a hard surface (preferably anodized) pan with a rounded side. An omelet pan can be any size. A 9-inch pan yields a fluffy, thick creation; a 12-inch pan delivers a thin, almost crepelike dish.

Don's Basic Omelet

2 or 3 large eggs
1 tablespoon water
nonstick cooking spray

Gently beat eggs to break yolks, but don't blend completely. Add water and beat until froth begins to build. Spray pan and heat over medium heat. Pour eggs into pan slowly, allowing them to spread evenly across bottom of pan. Rotate pan gently to build a lip around edge. Cook slowly until top is firm and bottom is lightly browned. Add desired extras (meat, cheese, veggies, or whatever) to half of omelet. Loosen omelet from pan by gently sliding spatula underneath. Slowly slide omelet half out of pan onto plate, then flip remaining half over to close omelet. The heat of the eggs will melt the cheese and heat veggies and meat. Serves 1.

☛ *Tip: Take filling ingredients out of the icebox or fridge well ahead of time so they can warm to "room" temperature. If you forget, warm the fillings (except cheese) in the frying pan while it's preheating.*

Omelet à la Terry Rodriguez

1 tablespoon each olive oil, vegetable oil
$1/2$ medium potato, sliced (leave skin on)
$1/2$ medium onion, chopped
2 or 3 eggs
small handful pimento-stuffed olives, sliced
pepper to taste

Heat frying pan over medium heat. Heat oils in pan and cook potato and onion until tender. Remove veggies from pan with slotted spoon. Beat eggs and olives together with pepper. Pour in pan and cook over low heat until partially cooked. Slide spatula around the edges periodically to loosen from pan. Add onion and potato and fold omelet. Cook until firm. Serves 1.

You can, of course, cook your eggs in a variety of ways, from frying to poaching. (If you can't figure out fried eggs by now, well . . .)

Did you know you can poach eggs in a frying pan? Serve them on toast over a slice of ham and cheese, if you like.

Poached Eggs

$1^1/2$ cups water
4 eggs
2 teaspoons vinegar (cider, wine, or white)

Boil water in frying pan. Add vinegar and gently break eggs into lightly rolling water. As eggs solidify, roll them with a serving spoon to keep tendrils from spreading. When cooked to taste (Don likes about 4 to 5 minutes), remove from pan with slotted spoon.

Then again, eggs of another sort can include the easiest way we know to combine scrambled eggs and maple syrup.

French Toast

> 4 to 6 slices bread, slightly stale
> 4 eggs
> nonstick cooking spray
> maple syrup, jelly, or powdered sugar (optional)

Preheat frying pan. In a bowl, beat eggs. Dip bread slices (you can make them stale by just leaving them out in the air for about a half hour) and soak in egg mixture until thoroughly moist. Spray pan and cook one or two slices (depending on pan size) at a time. Brown well and cook thoroughly before flipping. Remove to plate and serve with favorite topping.

■ CAKES: GRIDDLE, PAN, AND OTHERWISE

Sometimes eggs just aren't what you want. You want an old-fashioned sailor's breakfast that'll stick to your ribs all day long. Flatboat crews on the Ohio called them johnnycakes. Whatever you name them, they're fun to cook and sooo good to eat.

Pancakes in a Sack

> 1½ cups all-purpose flour
> 2 teaspoons white or yellow cornmeal
> 2 teaspoons brown sugar
> ¾ teaspoon salt
> 1½ teaspoons baking soda
> 2 teaspoons baking powder
> 2 eggs
> 2 cups milk
> nonstick cooking spray

Mix the dry ingredients at home and place in a bag. In the galley, mix all ingredients together in bowl using a whisk until blended but still lumpy. Preheat and then spray frying pan. Spoon batter into pan, enough for 2 or maybe 3 pancakes. Fry until golden brown; flip and cook other side. Serve with maple syrup and bacon or sausage.

You can also take the basic pancake recipe and add blueberries, bananas, or other fruit. And then there are some really ambitious ways to present the basic pancake.

Apple Pancakes

2 to 3 apples, cored, peeled, and chopped
$1/2$ cup maple syrup
2 tablespoons butter or margarine
2 cups milk
2 eggs
1 tablespoon liquefied Crisco shortening
$3/4$ cup Bisquick
$1/2$ teaspoon cinnamon
$1/2$ teaspoon nutmeg

Combine apple, maple syrup, and butter in hot 12-inch frying pan over medium heat and cook until tender. Mix milk, eggs, Crisco, Bisquick, cinnamon, and nutmeg to make batter. Remove apples from frying pan (reserve liquid) and add fruit to batter. Spoon batter into hot frying pan—you will have one large pancake. Cover pan and reduce heat. When dry bubbles appear, turn once, cover, and cook until golden brown. Serve on platter with reserved liquid from apples. Serves 3 or 4, depending on appetite.

LUNCH & DINNER

Galley fare can be simple or complicated. Your choice. We'll just divide things up by protein source starting with fowl things.

■ POULTRY

You can substitute any type of bird in recipes calling for chicken as far as we're concerned—duck, pheasant, game hen, or turkey. Some have a stronger flavor than others, so consider that before substitutions are made. Also, if you're trying to lower your fat intake, use skinless white meat whenever possible.

There are actually a couple of ways you can go in terms of chicken. If you have adequate refrigeration, buy your chicken fresh (not previously frozen, unless it is going directly from the store to your cooler; DO NOT REFREEZE!). If you're not that cool, Tyson and Valley Fresh have recently introduced 7-ounce soft packages of precooked and diced chicken breasts that require no chilling and no cooking. Other producers will probably follow suit. These softpacks will yield two 3½-ounce servings (a bit small, but adequate). The recipes here (even those specifying "whole" chicken) will turn out fine using either source. Simply substitute the contents of one softpack for two chicken breasts. Canned chicken products are another possibility, but be aware they tend to have higher sodium counts than fresh chicken, which may impact some dietary restrictions, so it's worth checking the labels.

Given good-quality meat, poultry can make for some very interesting and satisfying meals.

☛ Note: Technically, a whole chicken breast really offers two servings. A whole breast looks something like a valentine heart. A single serving should be slightly smaller than your hand (or half a "heart"), weighing (boneless and skinless) about 4 to 6 ounces. Thus, when we specify "two chicken breasts," we are calling for two single-serving-size pieces.

Walnut Chicken

$^1/_4$ cup vegetable oil

1 cup walnuts

1 tablespoon cornstarch

2 tablespoons cold water

2 tablespoons soy sauce

2 boneless, skinless chicken breasts

1 packet reduced-sodium Wyler's MBT Chicken Broth

$^3/_4$ cup boiling water

1 cup precooked rice

Heat oil in frying pan over high heat. Fry walnuts lightly (do not brown). Remove walnuts and reserve 3 tablespoons of oil. Mix cornstarch, cold water, and soy sauce with reserved oil. Pour into hot pan, add chicken, and brown. Dissolve contents of broth packet in boiling water and add to pan. Stir in walnuts. Continue stirring until thick and serve over precooked rice. You could add slices of green pepper after browning chicken, if you like.

If you want an Asian flavor (you can even use a wok), there are a lot of different chicken dishes that will spice up your dinner.

Pods 'n' Birds

2 boneless chicken breasts (or softpack), cut in 1-inch pieces

$1/4$ cup cornstarch

1 egg white

2 tablespoons white wine

2 tablespoons peanut oil

4 mushrooms, sliced

$1/4$ pound fresh snow peas

$1/4$ teaspoon salt (optional)

$1/4$ teaspoon ginger

$1/4$ cup nuts (any kind)

$1/4$ cup watercress (optional)

1 cup precooked rice

Dredge chicken in cornstarch. Combine egg white and wine. Beat well and set aside. Heat 1 tablespoon of oil in frying pan until it smokes. Sauté mushrooms, snow peas, ginger, and salt (if desired) for 2 minutes. Remove from pan with slotted spoon. Add remaining oil to pan. Add chicken to egg-white mixture in bowl. Add to pan and sauté for about 2 minutes. Add nuts and any additional vegetables you like, such as watercress, and cook about 3 to 4 minutes more. Serve with rice.

Delhi Chicken with Rice

1 tablespoon vegetable oil

1 medium onion, chopped

2 boneless chicken breasts, cut in 1-inch cubes

1 tablespoon flour

$1/4$ teaspoon ginger

1 to 2 tablespoons curry powder (or to taste)

2 tablespoons honey

2 tablespoons soy sauce

2 chicken bouillon cubes

2 cups water

$3/4$ cup uncooked white rice

1 or 2 carrots, sliced

Heat oil in pan. Add onion and sauté until brown. Add chicken and brown. Sprinkle flour, ginger, and curry powder into pan and stir. Add honey, soy sauce, bouillon cubes, and water. Simmer for 5 minutes. Add rice and carrots. Stir and simmer uncovered for another 20 to 25 minutes.

The following is a variation on the previous recipe that presents a little different flavor.

Bombay Breast

2 boneless chicken breasts (or softpack), cut in 1-inch cubes

$1/4$ cup soy sauce

2 tablespoons lime juice

1 tablespoon honey

$1/4$ teaspoon curry powder

1 green pepper, chopped

1 red pepper, chopped

$1/2$ cup bean sprouts

1 tablespoon peanut oil

In a bowl, mix all ingredients except oil. Marinate for 20 minutes. Heat pan over high flame until very hot (a drop of water on pan surface should "dance"). Drain marinade. Stir-fry ingredients in pan for about 5 to 10 minutes or until chicken is cooked through and veggies are tender. If you wish to use the marinade as a sauce, you *must* (for food safety) bring it to a boil in the frying pan after the meat and vegetables are removed.

Then again, maybe your taste is more Mediterranean than Bengali.

Chicken Scallopine

2 boneless chicken breasts (or softpack), cut in 1-inch cubes

$^1/_4$ cup flour

salt and pepper to taste

1 egg

1 to 2 tablespoons olive oil

1 clove garlic, peeled and sliced

1 chicken bouillon cube

$^3/_4$ cup boiling water

$^1/_4$ cup dry red wine

4 mushrooms, sliced

2 cups precooked spaghetti or pasta

Place flour, salt, and pepper in plastic bag. In a bowl, beat the egg. Dip chicken into egg and then place in bag with flour. Shake until well coated. Heat oil in pan and sauté garlic until it begins to brown. Lower heat, add chicken, and sauté slowly until brown. Add bouillon cube, water, wine, and mushrooms. Simmer uncovered for 15 minutes. Add pasta and then heat through.

☛ *Tip: You can substitute veal cutlets for chicken and grape juice for wine.*

_____

Basil Chicken Scallopine

This recipe is identical to the previous one except that you substitute sliced fresh basil leaves (6 or 7, or as many as you like) for the garlic. To slice the leaves, stack them one on top of the other, gently roll the pile into a small cylinder (like a pencil), and carefully cut across the resulting tube. Do not brown them; wilt them in the hot oil for a brief moment just before adding the chicken for a more delicate flavor and aroma.

_____

Chicken Catch-a-Tory

$1/2$ pound boneless chicken (or softpack), white or dark pieces
salt and pepper to taste
garlic powder to taste
2 tablespoons olive oil
1 medium onion, sliced
1 medium green pepper, sliced
1 6-ounce can tomato paste
1 cup water
4 to 6 mushrooms, sliced
$1/4$ teaspoon oregano

Coat chicken with salt, pepper, and garlic powder. Heat oil in pan. Add chicken and brown. Remove chicken. Add onion and green pepper to pan and sauté until tender. Add tomato paste, water, mushrooms, oregano, and chicken. Cover and cook for 30 minutes over medium flame.

This recipe goes well with rice, rice cakes, or bread.

Hong Kong Bird, or Chicken Crunch

$1/2$ pound boneless chicken (or softpack), white or dark pieces
2 tablespoons peanut oil
$1/2$ cup orange juice
$1/2$ teaspoon ginger
$1/2$ cup raisins
1 6-ounce can water chestnuts, sliced
$1/2$ cup white wine
$1/2$ cup salted cashews
1 tablespoon cornstarch
2 tablespoons water

Heat oil in pan. Add chicken and brown. Reduce heat and add remaining ingredients except cashews, cornstarch, and water. Simmer for 30 minutes. Add cashews. Using whisk, mix cornstarch and water in cup and add as needed to thicken sauce.

How many peanut butter sandwiches have you faced? And how many times have you stared at that jar and wondered if there was something else you could do with it? Here's one for you. It can be served with quinoa or another grain.

Sticky Chicken

$1/2$ pound boneless chicken breast (or softpack), cut in 1-inch cubes

$1/4$ cup peanut butter

1 tablespoon honey

2 tablespoons soy sauce

$1/8$ teaspoon garlic powder

1 tablespoon lemon juice

$1/4$ teaspoon cayenne pepper

2 medium onions, chopped

1 cup water

1 tablespoon ketchup

salt and pepper to taste

Combine all ingredients in pan and cook over medium flame until chicken is cooked.

You'll notice that we tend to specify boneless chicken. It really doesn't make any difference, but this way you don't have to deal with chicken bones when you're done eating.

Once in awhile, pack some butter instead of oils. It's great for its milk-fat content, as in the following sauce.

Saucy Chicken

White Sauce

2 tablespoons butter

2 tablespoons flour

1 cup milk (or powdered milk and water in 1:3 ratio)

In pan, melt butter over low heat. Blend in flour and gradually add milk and cook, stirring constantly, for 5 minutes until sauce is smooth. Set aside in cup, clean pan, and continue with the following.

2 boneless chicken breasts

1 teaspoon salt

$1/4$ teaspoon white pepper

$1/4$ cup ($1/2$ stick) butter

$1/2$ cup dry white wine

$3/4$ cup white sauce

1 medium green pepper, cut in strips

Rub chicken with salt and pepper. In preheated pan over medium flame, melt half the butter and lightly brown chicken. Add wine and white sauce. Cook 20 minutes. Add remaining butter and green pepper. Cook until hot, but do not burn sauce. Can be served with rice or noodles.

But just maybe your taste is for something a little redder.

Chicken Papri-Crash

$1/2$ pound boneless chicken (or softpack), white or dark pieces

salt and pepper to taste

garlic powder to taste

2 tablespoons peanut oil

1 medium onion, thinly sliced

1 medium green pepper, cut in strips

1 medium tomato, chopped

2 chicken bouillon cubes

1 cup water

1 tablespoon paprika (Hungarian is best)

$1/2$ cup uncooked Minute Rice

Rub chicken with salt, pepper, and garlic powder. To preheated pan, add oil and chicken. Brown chicken on both sides. Add onion and green pepper and cook for 2 to 3 minutes. Add tomato, bouillon cubes, and water. Bring to boil. Add paprika and stir. Cover and cook for 10 minutes over medium heat. Five minutes before serving, add Minute Rice to simmering sauce. Cook for 1 minute and let stand 4 minutes, covered (make sure all rice is soaking in sauce, or else you'll find some unexpected crunch).

Apples are some of the easiest fruits to take with you on your cruise and are easily stowed in a small net hanging under a side deck, where they get plenty of air.

Hens 'n' Apple

1 Cornish hen, quartered
2 tablespoons vegetable oil
$^1/_2$ teaspoon garlic powder
1 small onion, chopped
salt and pepper to taste
$^1/_4$ cup dry white wine
1 medium apple (McIntosh, Granny Smith, or other tart apple), chopped

Preheat pan, add oil, and brown hen. Sprinkle with salt, pepper, and garlic powder, then add onion. Add wine and cover. Simmer for 10 minutes. Stir in apple and cover again. Cook another 10 minutes or until apples are quite soft. Try adding a few small white potatoes when you pour in the wine.

Going back to butter as a substitute for oils, here's an old favorite.

Chicken à la King

$^1/_3$ cup water
2 boneless chicken breasts (or softpack), diced
2 tablespoons butter
2 tablespoons flour
1 cup milk
$^1/_4$ teaspoon salt (optional)
pepper to taste
1 small green pepper, chopped
3 mushrooms, sliced
1 egg yolk, slightly beaten

In preheated pan, heat water to rolling boil. Place chicken in water to poach. Stir meat constantly to avoid sticking. When tender (no more than 4 or 5 minutes), remove chicken and dispose of water. Return pan to flame and melt butter. Sauté green pepper and mushrooms. Sprinkle veggies with flour and stir. Add milk and seasonings. Cook until thick, stirring constantly. Add chicken and egg yolk. Cook another 10 minutes over medium heat, stirring to keep from scorching. Serve over bread, biscuits, or other grain.

Triple C (Chicken, Carrots, and Corn)

 2 boneless, skinless chicken breasts
 2 tablespoons olive oil
 3 cloves garlic, crushed
 1 cup chicken broth
 $1/4$ teaspoon dried basil
 $3/4$ cup fresh carrots, sliced
 $3/4$ cup fresh, uncooked corn cut from cob
 2 tablespoons butter or margarine
 2 tablespoons flour
 $1/2$ cup water

Warm pan over medium flame. Add oil and garlic, cooking about 1 minute. Add chicken and brown 5 minutes per side. Add chicken broth and sprinkle basil over chicken. Poach for about 10 minutes, turning once. Add carrots and corn. Simmer until tender, adding water (or broth) as needed. Be careful, though, not to create a chicken stew. Using slotted spoon, remove chicken and veggies to covered serving dish. Increase heat to bring remaining broth mixture to boil. Melt butter in the simmering broth. Mix flour and water in cup and gradually add to pan, stirring quickly to avoid lumps. Serve sauce over plated chicken and vegetables.

Basil Wrathboned Chicken

2 boneless chicken breasts
$^1/_4$ cup flour
salt and pepper
$^1/_4$ cup olive oil
1 tablespoon green onion, chopped
$^1/_2$ cup fresh green beans, sliced
1 chicken bouillon cube
$^1/_2$ cup water
1 large tomato, chopped
$^1/_2$ teaspoon basil
1 tablespoon vegetable oil
1 cup precooked pasta
Parmesan cheese (optional)

Combine flour, salt, and pepper in bowl. Dredge chicken in flour mixture. Preheat pan and add half the olive oil. Add chicken and cook until tender. Discard oil. Add remaining olive oil to pan. Sauté onions and beans for 1 to 2 minutes. Add bouillon cube, water, tomato, and basil. Simmer uncovered for 5 minutes. Remove from pan. Add vegetable oil and precooked pasta to pan to reheat it. Serve chicken over pasta and sprinkle with Parmesan.

There are probably a thousand ways to clog your arteries with fried chicken. Let's do it simply and then have some fun. For safety's sake, these recipes should be used only when you are in a calm anchorage or in your slip, where you don't have to worry about someone cruising by and throwing a large wake that will rock your boat violently. Also, this is where your frying pan with high straight sides really earns its keep. A high-sided pan rather than one with curved sides ensures that the hot oil, including spatters, stays in the pan. It's not only a question of protecting yourself, but also one of keeping the hot oil away from your lighted stove burner. Galley fires are not pleasant.

Alternatively, if you're using a portable grill or stove to cook on the dock, be *careful not to try the next few recipes in the rain. Water in hot oil spatters furiously and can easily burn you. For that matter, be careful with hot oil even when it's not raining. Hot oil can cause some very nasty burns.*

Square-One Fried Chicken

> 1 egg
> $\frac{1}{2}$ cup milk
> salt and pepper to taste
> $\frac{1}{2}$ cup flour
> $\frac{1}{2}$ pound chicken (white or dark pieces)
> $\frac{1}{3}$ cup vegetable oil

Beat together egg, milk, salt, and pepper. Roll chicken pieces in flour, then in egg mixture, then in flour again. Preheat pan and heat oil until it bubbles. Be very careful! Brown chicken on all sides. Cover and cook over low flame for 20 minutes or until chicken is cooked through. If using a precooked chicken product, you can eat the nuggets after the covering is crisp. Remove chicken to plate and blot with paper towel to absorb excess oil. Serve with fresh green salad or coleslaw and cold beer!

Chicken Gone Crackers

Same as the previous recipe, but substitute $\frac{1}{4}$ cup crushed saltine crackers and $\frac{1}{4}$ cup white cornmeal for the flour. Add about $\frac{1}{4}$ teaspoon of garlic powder to egg mixture. Cook as above.

Luigi's Fried Chicken

This time you keep the flour, but add $\frac{1}{4}$ teaspoon garlic powder to the egg mixture and $\frac{1}{2}$ teaspoon oregano to the flour. Also, you cook in olive oil. You can add some basil to the flour, as well.

Batter-Up Fried Chicken

Combine egg mixture and flour together to make a batter. Add flour as needed to thicken so you get an even, deep coating on your bird. You'll also want extra oil; maybe increase it to 1/2 cup. Cook uncovered.

Mr. Natural's Fried Fowl

2 eggs
1/2 cup milk
1/4 cup flour
1/2 cup rolled oats, Red River cereal, or other grain
salt and pepper to taste
1/2 pound chicken (white or dark pieces)
1/2 cup peanut oil

Mix eggs, milk, flour, and grain together to form a batter. If batter seems thin, add more flour. Rub salt and pepper on the chicken and then dip it in the batter. Preheat pan and add oil. When oil bubbles, place chicken in pan and cook thoroughly, turning periodically until tender. Remove chicken to paper towel.

Cheesy Fried Chicken

1 egg
1/4 cup milk
1/4 teaspoon salt (optional)
1/4 teaspoon pepper
1 tablespoon Parmesan cheese
1/2 pound chicken (white or dark pieces)
1/2 cup flour
2 tablespoons butter or margarine
3 to 4 tablespoons olive oil
3 tablespoons lemon juice
2 teaspoons whole pine nuts
1 teaspoon fresh chopped parsley

Beat egg, milk, salt, pepper, and cheese. Dredge chicken in flour, dip it in egg mixture, and dredge it in flour again. Preheat pan and add butter and oil; heat until bubbling. Add chicken and brown on all sides. Lower heat and cook until chicken is tender (maybe 20 minutes). Remove chicken. To remaining oil in pan, add lemon juice, pine nuts, and parsley. Cook for 1 minute or until nuts are browned. Pour over chicken.

Here's a foreign food that's fun to make, fun to eat, and we think it's good for you. You can cook veggies, beef, or poultry this way.

Tempura Batter

1 egg
$\frac{1}{4}$ teaspoon salt (optional)
$\frac{1}{4}$ teaspoon sugar
$\frac{1}{2}$ cup cold water
$\frac{1}{3}$ cup flour

Beat eggs, salt, and sugar in bowl until frothy. Continue beating while adding cold water. Add flour and mix well, but don't overdo it. The batter holds best if you can keep it cold, say by placing it in another bowl of chilled water.

You'll need a lot of oil for tempura, and you'll almost certainly want to use a high-sided pot. Depending on the size of your pot, you might need as little as 1/2 cup peanut oil to as much as 2 cups. The rule is that you need enough oil so that whatever you fry in it floats. Same holds if you're using a wok. Then heat the oil until it bubbles.

You can cook any vegetable—from potatoes to squash, from broccoli to carrots—and any meat in this batter. Just make sure that your pieces (especially for solid veggies such as carrots) are not too thick to fry.

Chicken Tempura

2 boneless chicken breasts, cut in strips
2 large carrots, peeled and thinly sliced
1 large green pepper, cut in thin strips (julienned)
1 small Vidalia (sweet) onion, sliced 1/8 inch thick
1 cup precooked rice (optional)

Dip chicken and veggies into the batter a few pieces at a time and add to hot oil. Cook until lightly browned (make sure chicken is cooked through!). Remove to a paper towel to drain. Remove crumbs from oil with slotted spoon before adding next batch. Serve alone or with rice. Soy sauce is a nice touch.

■ VEGETABLES

There are a lot of folks who like to take a day off from eating meat every once in awhile. Maybe a main dish that centers around something green. It's a nice change of pace and eliminates the need (usually) for radical refrigeration. Just remember that vegetables bruise easily and, when dinged, spoil fast.

Eggplant Ragout

    1 small eggplant, peeled and julienned

    1 medium tomato, chopped

    1 small onion, chopped

    1 small green pepper, chopped

    1 6-ounce can tomato paste

    $1/2$ cup water

    salt and pepper to taste

    $1/4$ teaspoon paprika

    $1/4$ teaspoon basil

    Parmesan cheese (optional)

Put everything in a large frying pan. Stir and simmer until veggies are soft and sauce is thick, about 30 minutes. You might also add some Parmesan cheese or seasoned bread-crumbs to thicken the base.

Many times, the veggie role in a meal is as a side dish. Remember that you can usually cook any vegetables you want in the side of your frying pan—accepting the fact that you may, from time to time, have to live with a bit of unusual sauce as a complement to your greens.

Road House Hash Browns

1 tablespoon peanut oil
1 medium onion, chopped
1 large potato, thinly sliced (leave peel on)
salt and pepper to taste
leftover bacon, salami, or other meat, diced (optional)

Heat pan over medium flame and add oil. Sauté onions in oil until tender. Add all other ingredients and continue cooking until potatoes begin to stick to pan. This goes well with red meats, but fits any meal. A real belly-warmer.

This is another hash-brown variation. Add a couple of eggs for a real scrambler!

Tennessee Stir-Fry

1 medium onion, diced
1 medium green pepper, julienned
1 tablespoon corn oil
3 medium russet potatoes, peeled and thinly sliced
$1/2$ pound precooked turkey ham, diced
black pepper to taste

Over medium flame, heat oil and cook onion and pepper until soft. Add potatoes and brown. Add ham and stir everything until hot.

Bay of Fundy Fries

2 large potatoes, cut in $1/4$-inch spears (leave skin on)
$1/4$ cup vegetable oil
1 tablespoon Tabasco sauce
seasoned salt (optional)

Place potatoes and Tabasco sauce in plastic bag and shake to coat. Heat oil in pan. Add potatoes and cook for 3 to 5 minutes, stirring occasionally to prevent sticking. Remove with slotted spoon. Drain on cloth or paper towel. Sprinkle with seasoned salt.

Spuds 'n' Peppers

1 jalapeño pepper, diced (watch it, these are potent)
2 tablespoons oil, butter, or margarine
1 medium green pepper, thinly sliced
1 medium red pepper, thinly sliced
2 large potatoes, peeled and thinly sliced
salt and pepper to taste
garlic powder to taste

First, you have to roast the jalapeño pepper: Devise a type of rack in the frying pan—maybe a piece of aluminum foil—to keep the jalapeño off surface of pan. Place jalapeño on rack, cover, and roast for 5 to 10 minutes over high flame. Remove pepper from pan and peel. Place oil in pan and heat. Add all vegetables and fry until browned and crispy. Add seasonings as desired.

☞ Tip: To make a complete meal, push the vegetables to the side of the pan and cook a boneless chicken breast in the juices for about 10 minutes, flipping occasionally.

Parmy Shrooms 'n' Noodles

1 tablespoon peanut oil

5 mushrooms, diced

1 medium onion, diced

$^1/_2$ cup milk

$1^1/_2$ cups precooked noodles

$^1/_2$ cup ham, diced (optional)

$^1/_4$ cup Parmesan cheese

Heat frying pan over medium heat. Add oil and sauté vegetables until tender, but not brown. Drain oil. Add milk, noodles, ham, and cheese and toss over low heat for 1 to 2 minutes until mixture is hot.

Sunshine Squash

2 tablespoons peanut oil

1 medium onion, diced

1 large summer squash, diced

5 to 6 mushrooms, sliced or chopped

$^1/_4$ to $^1/_2$ teaspoon garlic powder

$^1/_4$ teaspoon pepper

salt to taste

Preheat frying pan over medium flame. Add oil and sauté onion until tender. Add squash and cook uncovered until desired tenderness (Don likes his "crisp-tender"). Add the mushrooms and seasonings and cook for 3 to 4 more minutes.

Blanching vegetables at home is an easy way to make sure you have cooked vegetables on board. Usually, blanching works best with firm green vegetables such as beans, asparagus, broccoli, zucchini, and pea pods. But you can shorten your cooking time (and save stove fuel) with any frying-pan vegetable by taking a few minutes at home to blanch them and then repack them in a bag. They'll still be crispy, but well on their way to being cooked "just right."

To blanch, boil about 2 cups water (salt optional) in a pot. Place the desired vegetables in water and cook for 2 minutes—no more, no less. Drain immediately. Let cool and place in plastic bag. Chill in fridge and transfer to the cooler.

Here's a tasty way to use those home-blanched green beans.

McAuliffe's Green Beans

2 tablespoons vegetable oil
1½ cups green beans, sliced
3 ounces (or more) almonds, sliced

Heat frying pan over low flame. Add oil and let heat. Add almonds and fry gently (be careful not to burn them). Add beans and increase heat to medium. Toss beans and almonds together for about 1 minute—long enough for veggies to heat, but not long enough for almonds to burn.

Stir-Fry Vegetables

3 tablespoons peanut oil
2 cups mixed vegetables, chopped (green beans, pea pods, carrots, onions, mushrooms, green or red peppers)
2 tablespoons soy sauce
pepper to taste

Heat frying pan over high flame (drop of water on surface should "jump"). Add oil and let heat. Add vegetables and stir-fry for about 2 to 3 minutes. Add soy sauce and pepper. Toss and stir-fry for another minute. Serve over rice.

Potato Pancakes

2 large potatoes, peeled and grated

1 egg, beaten

1 tablespoon flour

$^1/_2$ teaspoon baking powder

2 tablespoons butter or margarine (or nonstick cooking spray)

Combine all ingredients except butter and form into flat cakes. Over medium flame, heat butter. Cook like regular pancakes, turning to brown both sides.

This dish can be used as an appetizer or as a side to a chili dish.

Quesadillas of Many Colors

2 soft flour tortillas

1 2- to 3-ounce can mild green chilis, sliced or diced

$^1/_4$ cup cheddar cheese, grated

$^1/_4$ cup jack cheese, grated

olive oil

mild salsa

sour cream

Place one tortilla on wax paper and cover with as many green chilis as you like. Sprinkle with cheeses and cover with other tortilla. Press gently. Warm pan and rub surface with oil (or use cooking spray). Place quesadilla in pan and cook until lightly browned. Flip and press with spatula. Brown and cook until cheese is melted (about 3 minutes, depending on heat). Remove, cut into wedges, and serve with salsa, sour cream, and (if desired) guacamole.

■ MEAT

Yes, you can substitute bear, venison, or buffalo for beef, if you wish. But whatever meat you use, make sure that it's high quality and well trimmed to eliminate waste (bones, gristle, and fat).

Although most of the following recipes specify particular cuts, you can usually substitute any grade. In recipes calling for hamburger or ground beef, we like to use 95 percent lean. You can use lower percentages, if you don't mind pouring off a good deal of fat. When all else fails, go with chopped, ground, sliced, or whole top sirloin. These cuts are lean and usually tender enough for most combinations.

Often, though, you'll start out cooking with hamburger. It's forgiving of beginners and weary boaters.

Hamburger Hash

$1/2$ pound ground beef

1 medium onion, diced

1 cup pinto beans (presoaked and packed in plastic bag)

$1/4$ cup ketchup

2 tablespoons brown sugar

$3/4$ cup water

1 beef bouillon cube

salt and pepper to taste

Brown beef and add onion. Cook until tender. Add all remaining ingredients. Stir mixture and simmer for 20 to 30 minutes or until sauce is smooth.

Purple Burger

$1/2$ pound ground beef

1 small onion, minced

$1/4$ cup pickled beets, diced

$1/2$ cup cooked potato, diced

$1/4$ teaspoon salt (optional)

$1/8$ teaspoon black pepper

1 tablespoon butter or margarine

In bowl, gently mix all ingredients except butter. Heat frying pan over medium flame. Melt butter in pan and spoon mixture onto hot surface. Flatten with spatula to about 1 inch. Cover and cook for 3 to 5 minutes or until browned. Flip once, cover, and finish cooking for another 5 minutes or until done. Divide and serve with hardtack or rye bread.

———————

Sometimes you might want to make a round meal rather than a square one in your frying pan. And what better way to celebrate a day on the water than with meatballs accompanied by hash browns? Or stir-fried green beans? Or raw sliced zucchini?

Soupy Meatballs

$1/2$ pound ground beef

$1/4$ cup seasoned breadcrumbs

$1/2$ medium onion, grated

salt and pepper to taste

2 tablespoons corn oil

2 cups water

2 packets beef-based soup mix (single-serving size)

1 cup noodles or macaroni (precooked saves time)

Combine meat, breadcrumbs, onion, and salt and pepper. Shape into meatballs about 1 to $1^1/2$ inches in diameter. Heat frying pan and add oil. Brown meatballs (roll them around to brown). Add water, noodles, and soup mix. Simmer for 5 to 10 minutes. If desired, add veggies such as diced fresh tomatoes to bubbling mix.

———————

Swedish Meatballs

$^1/_2$ pound ground sirloin

$^1/_4$ teaspoon sugar

1 egg

$^1/_4$ teaspoon sage

$^1/_4$ teaspoon allspice

$^1/_4$ teaspoon nutmeg

1 small onion, finely chopped

1 cup breadcrumbs

$^1/_3$ cup cold water

1 tablespoon vegetable oil

Mix all ingredients except oil together in bowl and knead well. Shape into 1-inch meatballs. Heat oil in frying pan and brown over medium flame. Roll meatballs around until cooked through. Cover and simmer for about 20 minutes, periodically rolling meatballs. If you like, add sliced potato and onion before simmering.

Gypsy Meatballs

Same as above, but substitute uncooked Minute Rice for breadcrumbs and substitute oregano and basil ($^1/_4$ teaspoon each) for sage, allspice, and nutmeg.

Everybody's mother has a recipe for goulash. Don's mom made hers with hamburger and elbow macaroni; John's mother subbed in rice.

Mom's Goulash

$1/2$ pound hamburger

salt and pepper to taste

1 large onion, diced

1 large green pepper, diced

$1/2$ teaspoon oregano

$1/4$ teaspoon garlic powder

$1/2$ teaspoon basil

1 teaspoon sugar

1 fresh tomato, cubed (optional)

1 6-ounce can tomato paste

1 cup water

$1^{1}/2$ cups precooked macaroni or rice

Heat frying pan over medium flame and brown meat until crumbly. Add salt, pepper, onion, and green pepper and sauté until veggies are soft. Drain any fat. Return to heat and add remaining ingredients except macaroni; stir until tomato paste is dissolved. Simmer for 10 minutes. Add macaroni or rice and stir until hot. Serve with Parmesan cheese and French bread.

Smoke Burgers

$1/2$ pound ground sirloin

$1/2$ small onion, chopped

$1/4$ teaspoon Liquid Smoke

ground pepper to taste

garlic powder to taste

1 tablespoon vegetable oil

Combine all ingredients except oil in bowl and knead by hand until well mixed. Heat frying pan over medium flame and add oil. Shape meat mixture into two $1/2$-inch-thick burgers and fry in pan to desired degree of doneness. If you're a cheeseburger nut, melt a thick slice of medium to sharp cheddar over each burger. Serve on a kaiser roll with salad on the side.

Sooner or later, you're going to want to get away from the ground-round side of life and step up to a different slice. That's when it gets to be fun.

Tokyo Teriyaki

3/4 pound sirloin steak, cut in 1-inch cubes
1/2 medium onion, chopped
1/4 teaspoon ginger
3 ounces teriyaki sauce
1/2 to 1 cup precooked rice
pineapple chunks

Combine steak, onion, ginger, and teriyaki sauce in bowl and marinate for 10 to 15 minutes. Heat frying pan and add steak and marinade. Cook until done. Add a little water, if necessary. Push meat and onions to one side of pan. Add precooked rice and heat through. About 1 minute before serving, add pineapple chunks and heat.

What trip would be complete without at least one dose of something to warm the insides and stretch the limits of your partner's patience?

Chili Blast

    1 pound stew beef or steak, cut into $^1/_2$-inch cubes
    1 small onion, chopped
    1 clove garlic, minced
    2 tablespoons vegetable oil
    1 15-ounce can corn, drained
    1 6-ounce can tomato paste
    1$^1/_4$ cups water
    2 chili peppers (mild or hot), seeded and chopped
    $^1/_4$ teaspoon salt (optional)
    spices to taste (cumin, coriander, or chili powder)
    one or more of following (optional): raisins, grapes, summer squash, zucchini,
        cactus ears

In frying pan, cook onion, beef, and garlic in oil until beef is browned. Add all other ingredients except optional ones. Bring to boil and reduce heat. Simmer covered for about 30 minutes. Add desired optional ingredients and simmer for about 10 more minutes or until meat is tender.

As for the next recipe, let's say thanks to a friend who Thai'd one on!

Bangkok Beef 'n' Peppers

    $^3/_4$ pound sirloin, cubed
    $^1/_4$ teaspoon garlic
    $^1/_2$ teaspoon ginger
    $^1/_2$ tablespoon sugar
    1 tablespoon soy sauce
    $^1/_4$ teaspoon cayenne pepper
    1 tablespoon vegetable oil
    1 medium onion, chopped

1 medium red pepper, cut in strips

1 beef bouillon cube dissolved in $3/4$ cup boiling water

$1/2$ cup mushrooms, sliced

1 teaspoon cornstarch

1 tablespoon water

$1^1/_2$ cups precooked rice

In bowl, combine beef, garlic, ginger, sugar, soy sauce, and cayenne pepper. Heat frying pan over high flame until very hot. Add oil and sauté onion and peppers until soft. Add beef and cook until browned. Stir often. Add bouillon mixture and mushrooms, and cook until sauce thickens. Mix cornstarch and water in cup with a whisk and add to thicken sauce. Serve with precooked rice. Some sliced fresh pineapple on the plate tastes great and helps cut the sting of this dish.

Hair-Raisin Curry Beef

$1/2$ cup boiling water

$1/2$ cup raisins

1 tablespoon olive oil

$3/4$ pound sirloin, cut in 1-inch cubes

1 medium onion, chopped

1 medium green pepper, chopped

$1/2$ tablespoon curry powder

$1/2$ teaspoon salt (optional)

$1/3$ cup unsalted peanuts

1 beef bouillon cube

In a dish or small bowl, pour boiling water over raisins and set aside. In a frying pan, add oil and brown meat and vegetables over medium heat. Drain oil. Add curry powder and mix well. Mix in salt (if desired) and nuts. Drain raisins (reserve juice) and add to meat mixture. To reserved raisin juice, add enough water to measure $1/2$ cup. Add this and bouillon cube to meat mixture and simmer for 15 minutes.

The following is not a recipe for the cholesterol-conscious. However, for a sunset-over-the-stern meal, there are few that can match this one for the fun of cooking and the sheer enjoyment of eating. You do have to be quick with this one. Have all of your ingredients prepped before you start to cook.

Stir-Fry Beef with Butter Sauce

Butter Sauce

>   2 ounces slivered almonds
>   1 green onion, chopped
>   1 tablespoon peanut oil
> $^1/_4$ teaspoon curry powder
>   1 stick butter (margarine is OK in a pinch)
>   juice of 1 lemon
>   salt and pepper to taste

Preheat frying pan over medium flame. Add oil and brown almonds and onion. Remove from heat and drain. Wipe pan clean. Return nuts and onion to pan and add remaining ingredients. Let butter melt, but do not brown. Stir until well mixed. Remove from pan and set aside in covered bowl.

>   2 tablespoons peanut oil
> $^3/_4$ pound beef, thinly sliced
> $^1/_3$ cup green peppers, chopped
> $^1/_3$ cup red peppers, chopped
> $^1/_3$ cup mushrooms, sliced
> $^1/_2$ teaspoon salt (optional)
>   pepper to taste

Heat oil until it smokes. Add meat and quickly brown. Turn regularly to keep from sticking and burning. Add remaining ingredients and quickly stir-fry. Reduce heat and add butter sauce. Toss quickly to coat.

☛ *Tip: If you want a lower-fat version, replace the butter sauce with $^1/_4$ cup red wine. Or, omit the butter sauce and go for some soy sauce to make tongues really tingle. By the way, these variations all work well with rice. Remember, precook the rice at home and then pour the freshly cooked food over it to reheat.*

Soy Sauce Sirloin

$^1/_2$ pound sirloin, thinly sliced

$^1/_4$ cup peanut oil

5 green onions, sliced in 1-inch pieces

1 6-ounce can water chestnuts, sliced

1 medium green pepper, sliced

4 ounces dried pineapple chunks

2 tablespoons cornstarch

$^1/_4$ cup water

$^1/_4$ cup soy sauce

Preheat pan and add oil. Sauté beef in hot oil for about 30 seconds on each side. Add remaining ingredients except cornstarch, water, and soy sauce. Cook 4 to 5 minutes over medium flame. Meanwhile, dissolve cornstarch in water. Add cornstarch mixture and soy sauce to pan and stir until thickened.

Feel like a taste of the Old West?

Big John's Dixie-Fried Steak

$^3/_4$ pound steak, well marbled, cut into 2 pieces

2 tablespoons butter

$^3/_4$ cup water

$^1/_4$ cup flour

salt and pepper to taste

Preheat frying pan over medium flame and melt butter. Add meat and slowly fry steak. Reduce heat as needed to keep from sticking. After meat is cooked as you prefer, re-move from pan. Add water and slowly stir in flour to make gravy, carefully scraping pan to remove all meat drippings. Pour gravy over steak. Serve with Hash Browns (see page 62) or Fundy Fries (see page 63) and a vegetable side.

Take a hard left turn at Vladivostok to get to the next flavor classic.

Beef Stroganoff

$^3/_4$ pound steak (round or sirloin), cut in 1-inch cubes

3 tablespoons flour

$^1/_2$ cup onion, chopped

3 tablespoons corn oil

1 clove garlic, minced

$^1/_4$ teaspoon pepper

$^1/_4$ teaspoon paprika

5 mushrooms, sliced

$^1/_3$ cup dry red wine or sherry

1 packet dry creamed vegetable soup mix, reconstituted with water

4 ounces cream cheese

precooked noodles

Place beef and flour in plastic bag and shake to coat. Heat frying pan over medium to high flame. Add oil. Sauté onions and beef in oil until beef is uniformly browned. Add remaining ingredients except soup and cream cheese. Stir and let simmer for about 5 minutes. Add soup and simmer another 10 minutes. Slice in cream cheese and stir well. Dish out steaming hot over precooked noodles.

Here's a version of goulash that's sure to tantalize a few taste buds whenever it's served.

Protein-Buster Goulash

    nonstick cooking spray
    $1/2$ pound sirloin steak, cut in $1/2$-inch cubes
    2 medium onions, chopped
    2 stalks celery, sliced
    2 packages dry tomato soup mix (single-serving size)
    $1^1/2$ cups water
    salt, pepper, and paprika to taste
    1 15-ounce can red kidney beans, drained
    flour

Spray pan and heat over medium to high flame. Add meat and brown until done. Add onions, celery, soup mix, and water. Simmer for 30 minutes. Add beans and seasonings. Thicken sauce with flour as needed. With all the beef and beans, you won't run short on protein. Serve this recipe with bread, and you'll have a meal you can really wrap yourself around.

DESSERT

We'll be honest. The frying pan isn't the easiest thing to use if you're trying to cook dessert. So here's our favorite fruit cup recipe.

Coconuts to You Fruit Cup

    1 orange, cubed

    1 apple or pear, cubed

    1 banana, sliced (optional)

    $1/4$ cup flaked coconut

    1 tablespoon sugar (optional)

Mix fruit, coconut, and sugar (if desired) and let rest in a covered dish for 30 minutes. Eat with great joy.

Many cultures feature pancakes as a favorite dessert. They're usually thin, sweet, and covered with marvelous fruit preserves or powdered sugar. Any pancake batter mix can serve the purpose, but add more water or milk than suggested because you want a thin batter to give you delicate, thin pancakes.

Don is half-Swedish, and offers this family favorite from the Old Country. If you're French, you'll know these as crepes; to Don, they're plättar.

Plättar

1 egg
$^2/_3$ cup milk
dash of salt (optional)
1 tablespoon sugar
$^1/_4$ cup flour
1 tablespoon vegetable oil

Beat egg well. Add milk, salt, sugar, flour, and oil. Mix thoroughly. Heat oil in frying pan. Cook pancakes on both sides. If batter is too thick, add a little more milk. These pancakes should be very thin. Serve with powdered sugar or strawberry preserves.

the
Pot

Although the recipes for the frying pan were designed for quick cooking, the ones for the pot are meant to be a bit slower to finish, allowing tougher meats to tenderize, pungent flavors to mellow, and tasty sauces to blend into a savory meal.

Meals built in the pot offer a unique taste experience. Certainly, the pot has traditionally been a world of stews and soups. But with a little extra effort and creativity, you can cruise the Adriatic or contemplate the Big Muddy when you put the 2-quart pot on the burner.

BREAKFAST

Getting breakfast out of the pot is one way to enjoy a hot first meal of the day when you're under way. But if you're in a sailboat and the water is rough, you might try heaving-to until the meal is finished. *Sea Sparrow* once had a wave slap her stern unexpectedly, causing a freshly filled bowl of hot cereal to jump from the countertop, flip upside down, and empty its contents onto one of our hands, causing a serious burn despite getting ice on the hand quickly.

Take a look at some of these fast favorites. These recipes serve two unless otherwise noted.

■ CEREALS

Cereals and other grain dishes are an easy way to get started and give you a lot of get-up-and-go. But you have to build a complete and balanced supply of nutrients. Don't forget the fruit and milk.

Oatmeal Extraordinaire

$1^1/_2$ cups water

$^1/_8$ teaspoon salt (optional)

$^2/_3$ cup old-fashioned oatmeal or steel-cut oats

$^1/_4$ cup raisins

2 tablespoons brown sugar

$^1/_4$ cup walnuts

Over a medium flame, bring the water and salt (if desired) to a boil. Add oats, stirring slowly to prevent lumping. Cook for 5 minutes (15 minutes for steel cut) or until all water is absorbed. Add raisins and cook for another 2 to 3 minutes, stirring occasionally. When ready to eat, stir in brown sugar and walnuts.

Cinnamon-Orange Cream of Wheat

2 cups water

$^1/_8$ teaspoon salt (optional)

$^1/_2$ cup Cream of Wheat (original, not quick)

1 teaspoon cinnamon

1 6-ounce can mandarin orange segments, drained

Over a medium flame, bring water and salt (if desired) to a boil. Add cereal, stirring to prevent lumping. Cook for 5 minutes, making sure not to burn cereal. Just before you're ready to eat, add cinnamon and oranges.

Of course, you can add just about anything you want to a cooked grain mixture. Just follow package directions and then let your imagination run wild. Some great taste combinations are apple chunks (dried or fresh), cinnamon, and nuts; dates and brown sugar; real maple syrup (needs no more help); and applesauce and sliced strawberries. Most of these additions require no cooking. Just put them in when you're ready to eat. Some, such as raisins and apples, need a few minutes in the mix to soften and warm up.

There are at least a dozen different commercial hot cereals to choose from. Look for bulk cereals at better markets that cater to quality-conscious consumers. You'll save a lot of money by eliminating the marketing and packaging. For instance, by buying in bulk, you can get steel-cut oats for around 79 cents per pound. The 10-ounce aluminum can sells for more than $4. By the way, many cold cereals, such as Grape Nuts and Shredded Wheat, can be cooked to make an early-morning tummy warmer.

Some of the cereals labeled "instant" or "quick" sacrifice some of the taste of the slower-cooking versions, though. Take the time (an extra 5 minutes or so) to cook up a mix that's really satisfying and packed with energy. You should also be aware that instant cereals often contain a lot more salt than you might want, especially if you're on a restricted sodium diet. Compare the 0 milligrams of sodium in a ½ cup (dry) serving of Old Fashioned Quaker Oats versus the 170 milligrams in a single-serving package of Quaker Instant Oatmeal Apples & Cinnamon.

■ MORNING BEVERAGES

We like coffee. Steaming hot, strong coffee. And we're not fanatics who insist that the only real coffee has grounds and egg shells floating in it. To get around the need to deal with a coffeepot, try using a small cook pot with a tea ball to contain the coffee grounds. Makes cleanup a whole lot easier. Of course, if you want to bring a percolator . . .

Hearty Crew Brew

2 tablespoons fresh-ground coffee (auto-drip or finer grind)

2 cups water

1 tablespoon sugar

1 teaspoon cinnamon

Bring water to boil. Spoon coffee into tea ball and add to boiling water. Let brew for 4 to 5 minutes. Remove tea ball. Add sugar and cinnamon. Makes 2 cups. Serve with milk, cream, or whitener if you prefer. Substitute some nutmeg for the cinnamon, if you wish. And if you want to go mocha, substitute unsweetened cocoa for cinnamon.

■ EGGS AND MEAT

About any way you can cook an egg in a frying pan, you can do in a pot—a bit differently, but cooked nonetheless. It's just more interesting when you go beyond the eggs and start adding meat, for instance. And that's where you have to change the way you think about how you cook meat.

For many people, meat isn't properly prepared until there's a charred layer to prove that it passed the trial by fire. But think Asian for a moment. Meat that has been steamed, not unlike dim sum, is just as well done as if it were stuck to your frying pan two or three times.

All you need is a vegetable steamer, about ½ cup of boiling water, and a cover for your pot to fix most cuts of meat. However, it's critical that the meat is thawed, especially if it's fresh instead of precooked or left over. Otherwise, you might end up with sausage or steak that is too rare or even dangerously undercooked.

As with all foods, make sure your meat hasn't spoiled before you cook it. You usually can't tell whether meat is spoiled just by looking at it, though certainly an "off" smell should tell you something's wrong. But sometimes meat can be bad and not give off any telltale aroma. When in doubt, toss it and open a can of beans. Better a meatless meal than risking food poisoning.

Another caution about steaming involves handling the utensils and steering clear of the steam. You can get an incredibly nasty burn from steam. Never place the steamer in a pot of boiling water. Always start with everything cold: The

The versatile vegetable steamer.

meat, the steamer, the pan, the water, and even the stove. When you remove the steamer from the pan, carefully lift the cover off away from your face. The first thing out of the pot will be live steam (that's steam under pressure—and it's a lot hotter than 212°F). Then, let everything cool off for a few moments before you move in with your hot-pot tongs to remove the steamer.

And now for the recipes.

Sausage Links

uncooked or brown 'n' serve links, thawed

Place links on steamer. Pour $1/2$ cup water in pan. Put steamer in pan and cover. Over medium flame, bring water to boil. Time cooking from when water boils; uncooked links get 10 minutes, brown 'n' serve just 5.

Ham Sticks

4 ounces cooked ham, cut into 4-inch sticks

Steam until piping hot (about 5 to 8 minutes). You can substitute Spam, but the consistency of the cooked product will be different.

Soy Sauce Steak Sunrise

$1/3$ cup soy sauce
2 tablespoons honey
$1/2$ pound sirloin or other lean steak, thinly sliced
$1/2$ cup cold water

Mix soy sauce and honey, and marinate steak in it for 15 minutes. Discard marinade. Place meat on steamer and put in pot with water. Cover and bring water to boil. Cook meat for 3 minutes (rare) to 6 or 7 minutes (well done).

A.M. Sausage Burrito

4 flour tortillas
2 tablespoons peanut oil
1 cup water
$^{1}/_{2}$ pound ground sausage
4 eggs
diced green pepper and onion (optional)

Rub oil on one side of each tortilla. Roll loosely and place on steamer. Place steamer in pan, add water, and bring to boil. Heat tortillas for about 1 minute. Remove pan from heat and remove cover. After steam clears, remove tortillas and place half of sausage meat in each tortilla on nonoiled side. Fold tortillas over meat so they resemble small pillows. Place back on steamer with folded part down. Bring water level back to 1 cup and place steamer inside pan. Cover and bring to boil over medium heat. Put eggs alongside tortillas on steamer to hard-boil. Time for 15 minutes after water boils. To spice up the burrito, add some diced green pepper and onion to meat before placing in tortillas.

———————

A great staple of any outdoor breakfast is the common chicken egg, though you can also use duck or goose eggs to fill out your morning plate.

Many of us think of eggs and frying pans as inseparable. Unfortunately that's too often the case, especially when we forget the butter, margarine, or cooking spray. But eggs in a pot on board ships have a noble history, reaching back into the smoky past of cast-iron cauldrons in a rolling galley as the cook tried to build a breakfast for the captain's table.

You can always treat your pot like a frying pan and make scrambled eggs, but be adventurous and try some of these recipes that turn the benefits of the pot to your eggs' advantage.

Hard-Boiled Eggs

4 large eggs
3 cups water
$1/4$ teaspoon salt

Pour water in pot with salt (if desired). Bring water to boil over medium-to-high flame. Reduce heat so water is just barely bubbling. Add eggs. Maintain flame so that water keeps boiling very slowly. Cook eggs too fast and they'll crack and ooze. Boil for about 5 to 7 minutes. Remove eggs with spoon and set aside to cool (soak in bowl of cold water). Peel and eat.

Hard-boiled eggs are versatile. You can peel and eat them as is. You can slice and sprinkle them with salt and pepper, grated cheese, diced chives or onions, or pine nuts and Parmesan. You can also do a bit more with hard-boiled eggs while still in the pot.

Eggs à la Goldenrod

4 hard-boiled eggs
$1/3$ cup flour
$3/4$ cup milk
$1/2$ to 1 cup water
white pepper
4 slices bread

Peel eggs and separate yolks from whites. Slice whites and set aside. Over a medium flame, heat milk in pot. Do not boil. In a bowl, add water a bit at a time to flour to make a paste. Slowly add paste to milk to make white sauce (stir as mixture thickens). Add sliced egg whites. Add white pepper to taste. Heat mixture through and spoon over bread. Mash yolks and sprinkle over top.

The most popular way to cook eggs in a pot, besides boiling them, is poaching them. Poaching eggs like a pro isn't hard; it just takes a bit of wrist action.

Poached Eggs

2 1/2 cups water
1/4 cup white vinegar
4 large eggs

Over a medium-to-high flame, bring water to a boil and add vinegar. With a spoon, stir liquid to create a whirlpool. Add eggs to whirlpool while continuing to swirl the water. This will roll the eggs and keep them from spreading out. Every 15 to 20 seconds, reverse the direction of the whirlpool by rocking the pan in the opposite direction. After about 3 minutes, remove eggs from pan. Serve over bread, rolls, or hot hash.

Poached eggs are the base for the king of all egg dishes: eggs Benedict. Simply speaking, this dish consists of poached eggs on top of sliced Canadian bacon and English muffins, covered with Hollandaise sauce. It's possible to make Hollandaise sauce in the galley, but you need a double boiler and a lot of patience. As an alternative, try substituting a spruced-up white sauce.

White Sauce for Poached Eggs

4 tablespoons flour
1/2 cup water
1/2 cup milk
2 tablespoons butter or margarine
salt and pepper to taste
Parmesan cheese (optional)

Mix flour and water in bowl to form paste. Heat milk in pot over medium flame. Add butter, stirring frequently until melted. Add flour mixture gradually to thicken sauce. Add salt and pepper. Continue to heat until sauce is thick. Set aside and cover. Serve over poached eggs placed on slice of ham or Canadian bacon on top of sliced English muffin to make mock eggs Benedict. For some added flavor, stir in a healthy dash of grated cheese.

LUNCH & DINNER

Turning your pot into a vat of earthly delights is easy if you're willing to take a little time. Cooking in a pot offers a totally different experience from cooking in a frying pan. The pot is a world of spices and sauces, of subtle differences in flavor, in which gentle nuances bring new blendings of taste to galley cuisine.

A pot-based meal should be cooked slowly, and this is where your flame tamer will earn its keep by diffusing your burner's heat over the bottom of the pot. You have to accept the fact that patience is the critical factor in melding meats, vegetables, seasonings, and liquids into more than an uninspired soup or stew. You can expect to spend 30 minutes or more cooking after the preparation is done. But the wait will be worth it.

That said, there are times when you may want to shorten the cooking time, if for no other reason than to conserve stove fuel. That's when a pressure cooker comes in handy. If the recipe cooking time—once all the ingredients have been added—is 30 minutes or longer, consider using the pressure cooker (use the timetables on pages 14–19 as guides). It's a good idea to write down what you do so you have a record of your cooking time, cooldown, etc., in case you have to make adjustments (e.g, if your first test is a bit over- or undercooked). We've also included some of our favorite pressure-cooker goodies (see pages 121–25).

■ POULTRY

Don prefers cooking with chicken breasts, but you can use any part of the bird—legs, thighs, whatever—in these recipes. You can substitute other poultry, if you like, but use caution. Turkey dark meat (legs, thighs) has a stronger flavor than chicken and will yield a different result. If you want to substitute, try turkey breast. Duck is quite greasy.

Chicken is great because it cooks quickly, it's lean (if you strip away the fat and go skinless), it's packed with nutrition, and it works with just about anything you can dig out of the fridge. And remember the various softpacks of pre-cooked chicken now on the market. You can substitute a 7-ounce softpack any time the recipe calls for boneless and cubed or diced meat.

☞ *Note: As mentioned in the previous chapter, two chicken breasts really means one whole breast (which looks something like a valentine heart) cut in half. Each piece will weigh 4 to 6 ounces.*

Icebox Chicken with Stuffing

$^1/_2$ pound boneless chicken breast (or softpack), cubed

3 tablespoons butter or margarine

1 medium onion, diced

$^1/_2$ cup green pepper, chopped

1 small tomato, diced

1 stalk celery, chopped

salt and pepper to taste

1 chicken bouillon cube

$^1/_2$ cup water

$^1/_2$ cup seasoned croutons, stuffing mix, or uncooked Minute Rice

$^1/_2$ teaspoon poultry seasoning, if you use Minute Rice

Over a medium flame, heat pot. Melt butter in pot and sauté vegetables until tender. Add chicken and cook until meat is done. Add salt and pepper, bouillon cube, and water. Continue cooking until cube dissolves. Add the croutons and stir into mixture until liquid is absorbed and croutons are soft. If you substitute Minute Rice for the croutons, cover the pot and let it sit off the heat for a few minutes.

☞ *Tip: If you are on a restricted-sodium diet, you can substitute a packet of reduced-sodium or sodium-free Wyler's MBT Chicken Broth for a chicken bouillon cube in any of these recipes.*

Here's a similar theme, but with a slightly different taste and look.

Potted Chicken

1 carrot, cut in chunks
$1/2$ stalk celery, sliced
$1/2$ medium onion, sliced
2 potatoes, diced
2 chicken bouillon cubes or 1 12-ounce can chicken broth
1 cup water (omit if using broth)
2 boneless chicken breasts
salt and pepper to taste
dried basil to taste

Place vegetables, bouillon, and water in pot. Bring to a boil over medium flame. Reduce heat and stir. Place chicken on top of veggies; season with salt, pepper, and basil. Cover and continue to cook over low flame for 30 minutes or until chicken is done. Add water as needed to keep broth level up.

―――――――――

The great thing about chicken is that it doesn't affect the flavor of the dish as strongly as red meats do. This lets you do some fun things with sauces and vegetables that might otherwise vanish in competition. The next is a major favorite.

Red and Green Chicken

$1/2$ pound boneless chicken breast (or softpack), cubed
2 tablespoons butter or margarine
1 small onion, diced
$1/2$ tablespoon paprika
$1/2$ teaspoon salt (optional)
pepper to taste
1 medium green pepper, diced
1 medium red pepper, diced
$3/4$ cup water
4 ounces cream cheese

Over medium flame, heat pot. Melt butter, add onions, and cook until browned. Add paprika and chicken and cook over low heat for about 20 minutes. Add water, salt, pepper, and remaining veggies. Cover and cook for another 15 to 20 minutes, stirring occasionally. Add cream cheese a lump at a time, letting each lump melt and mix into sauce. Serve with chunks of sourdough or other hearty bread. This dish really goes well with pasta, which can be precooked at home if you're just going out for a weekend. (Cook pasta, rinse with cold water, toss with a bit of olive oil, and refrigerate in a plastic bag. The sauce will reheat the pasta.)

Hot 'n' Steamy Chicken

    2 chicken legs
    1 large carrot, peeled and sliced
    1 large potato, peeled and sliced
    1 medium green pepper, sliced into spears
    $1/2$ cup sweet onion, in chunks
    1 tablespoon light brown sugar
    salt, pepper, and curry powder to taste
    3 tablespoons water

Place vegetables in pot. Combine curry powder, salt, pepper, and brown sugar. Coat chicken with this mixture. Place chicken on top of vegetables. Add water and cover pan. Cook over medium flame about 40 minutes. Check to make sure that water doesn't evaporate. Add more liquid if needed to avoid burning. Scrape veggies away from pan if they begin to stick, but don't stir mixture.

Calcutta Chicken

$^1/_2$ pound boneless, skinless chicken breast (or softpack), cubed

4 tablespoons butter or margarine

1 medium onion, finely chopped

1 stalk celery, finely chopped

$^1/_3$ cup flour

2 chicken bouillon cubes dissolved in $1^1/_2$ cups water

1 6-ounce can tomato juice

$^1/_2$ teaspoon Worcestershire sauce

1 teaspoon curry powder

precooked rice

Over medium flame, melt the butter and sauté vegetables until tender. Add chicken and cook thoroughly, stirring occasionally. Add flour and stir to mix. Add bouillon mixture immediately, and cook until sauce is smooth and thick. Add tomato juice, curry powder, and Worcestershire. Cover and simmer for 5 minutes. Serve over precooked rice. (Cook, rinse, stir in a little oil to keep it from clumping, and chill in a plastic bag.)

Barcelona Bird

$^1/_2$ pound boneless, skinless chicken breast (or softpack), cubed

2 tablespoons butter or margarine

1 large tomato, cubed

1 medium green pepper, diced

1 medium onion, chopped

1 6-ounce can tomato paste

$^3/_4$ cup water

$^1/_4$ teaspoon cayenne pepper

salt and pepper to taste

$^3/_4$ cup uncooked Minute Rice (optional)

$^1/_4$ cup black olives, diced (optional)

Over medium flame, heat pot and melt butter. Add chicken and cook for 10 minutes. Add veggies and sauté until chicken is tender. Add the remaining ingredients except rice and olives. Simmer sauce to very slow bubbling boil. Add rice and stir into mix. Cover and set aside for 5 minutes. Sprinkle with olives, if desired.

Keeping the international flavor, let's cross the Mediterranean and survey the Bay of Naples.

Colossal Chicken

> 1 tablespoon olive oil
> 2 boneless chicken breasts (or softpack), cut in chunks
> 1 medium onion, diced
> 1 clove garlic, crushed
> 3 large mushrooms, sliced
> 1 6-ounce can tomato paste
> 1 cup water
> 1 very ripe tomato, crushed
> $^{1}/_{2}$ teaspoon oregano
> $^{1}/_{4}$ teaspoon each basil, black pepper, and fennel seed
> 1 teaspoon sugar
> 1 tablespoon Parmesan cheese
> precooked spaghetti

Over medium flame, heat oil in pot. Brown chicken, turning to prevent sticking. Add vegetables and sauté until tender. Add remaining ingredients except pasta. Stir until tomato paste is incorporated. Reduce heat, cover, and cook for about 30 minutes. Balance seasonings as you wish. Serve with precooked spaghetti (for 2 servings, precook about 8 ounces of dry pasta).

☛ *Tip: For a powerful spaghetti sauce, try this without the chicken. Consider crumbling a bay leaf and dicing up green peppers to amplify the aroma and enhance the appearance.*

Friends have asked Don about the old Saturday night favorite, franks and beans. Hot dogs are an easy way out of having to think when you're cooking. However, the beans are another story.

Boston Basted Bird

 2 boneless, skinless chicken breasts

 6 strips thick-cut bacon

 1 12-ounce can baked beans, drained

 $\frac{1}{2}$ cup raisins

 1 tablespoon brown sugar

Wrap 3 strips bacon around each chicken breast. Heat pot over medium flame and brown meat. Cook for about 10 minutes, turning to keep from burning. Drain excess grease. Combine baked beans, raisins, and brown sugar. Pour mixture over chicken and bacon, making sure the meat is well covered. Cover pan and simmer over low heat about 25 minutes. Serve with brown bread.

☞ *Tip: This recipe can also be prepared as a casserole for the oven. Follow the recipe to the point of simmering over low heat. Instead, place it in oven pan, cover, and bake 1 hour at medium heat.*

Chicago-Style Chicken

 3 tablespoons flour

 1 tablespoon dry mustard

 1 teaspoon pepper

 2 boneless chicken breasts, cut in strips

 1 medium onion, chopped

 2 tablespoons vegetable oil

 2 cups milk

 1 tablespoon flour

 1 tomato, thinly sliced

 1 tablespoon chopped fresh parsley

 1 stalk celery, chopped

 1 dill pickle, chopped (optional)

Combine flour, mustard, and pepper in plastic bag. Place chicken in bag and shake to coat. In pot, heat oil and brown chicken, turning to avoid burning. Add onion and sauté until tender. Add flour to milk and add to pot, heating to a boil (do not burn). Add tomato, parsley, and celery. Reduce heat, cover, and cook for 20 to 25 minutes or until chicken is cooked. Stir to prevent sticking. Serve with hard roll and garnish with a chopped dill pickle, if desired.

————————

If you like mushrooms, you're sure to like this recipe.

Mushed Chicken

$1/2$ tablespoon vegetable oil

$3/4$ cup fresh mushrooms, sliced

1 medium onion, finely chopped

2 chicken bouillon cubes

1 cup water

2 boneless, skinless chicken breasts

oregano to taste

pepper to taste

$1/2$ cup uncooked Minute Rice

1 carrot, cut in thin curls

In pot over medium flame, heat oil and sauté mushrooms and onions. When vegetables are tender, add water and bouillon cubes. Bring to boil. Reduce heat and place chicken on top of vegetables. Season with oregano and pepper. Cover and cook for 35 minutes. Remove chicken and add rice. Stir to mix. Return chicken to pot. Drop carrots on top of all. Cover and cook another 5 minutes. Remove pot from stove and let sit 5 minutes before removing cover.

————————

This next dish goes great over noodles or French bread.

Chicken 'n' Green-Eyed Gravy

1 tablespoon vegetable oil

2 boneless chicken breasts (or softpack), cut in chunks

1 medium onion, chopped

$3/4$ cup water

1 chicken bouillon cube

1 15-ounce can peas, drained

salt and pepper to taste

flour and water to thicken

Heat pot over medium flame. Add oil and brown chicken. Add onion and cook until soft. Add all other ingredients except flour and cook for about 20 minutes. Add water as needed. Thicken gravy by making paste of water and flour and stirring in slowly to prevent lumps.

The search for flavor being the mother of invention, here's a quick and easy way to tickle your taste buds.

Creamed Chicken and Noodles

2 chicken bouillon cubes

$1^{1}/_{2}$ cups water

2 boneless chicken breasts (or softpack), cut in chunks

4 ounces cream cheese

1 15-ounce can peas, drained

2 tablespoons flour

1 red pepper, diced

1 cup precooked noodles or macaroni

In pot, bring bouillon cubes and water to boil. Add all other ingredients (add cream cheese a chunk at a time). Reduce heat, cover, and simmer for 30 minutes. Stir occasionally. Serve over precooked noodles.

This next recipe is about as simple as you can get in a pot. This is an old-timer, the roots of which are easily lost in the mists of the Ohio (or even the Thames).

Old-Fashioned Chicken Fricassee

> 4 chicken legs, disjointed
> 1½ cups water (approximate)
> 1 tablespoon flour
> 1 cup milk
> salt and pepper to taste
> precooked noodles or biscuits

Place chicken legs in pot and add just enough water to cover. Cook over medium flame for 35 to 45 minutes or until meat begins coming off bones. (There should be at least 1 cup of liquid left in pot.) Mix milk and flour together and add to pot. Bring to boil, stirring gently to prevent sticking. Add salt and pepper as desired. Serve over precooked noodles or biscuits. Fresh carrot sticks will fill out the meal.

☞ *Tip: To add some zest, slice a whole onion into the pot once the water boils. Do the same with a couple of carrots.*

Don't think you have to put your pot on the stove to make a sumptuous meal. Try this one on for size.

Tasty Chicken Salad

> ½ pound precooked boneless chicken (or softpack), diced
> ¼ cup honey
> ¼ cup vegetable oil
> juice of 1 lemon
> ½ teaspoon onion salt (optional)
> 2 stalks celery, diced
> 1 tablespoon Dijon mustard
> 1½ cups chop suey noodles

In pot, whisk together all ingredients except chicken and noodles. Add chicken and noodles and toss to coat with dressing.

■ SOUPS AND STEWS

When archaeologists examine the human record, they often evaluate civilizations based on the decorations found on potsherds turned up in the diggings. To us that says one thing: the ancients knew that the pot was more than just a water-gathering device. It was the center of the home; the symbol of the hearth that provided for all who clustered around.

Over the years, soups and stews have been a mainstay in the mariner's menu. The ingredients are relatively easy to carry and you can make a lot of soup quickly. The best time for a soup or stew is when the wind is cutting and you need warming up fast. Putting a pot of water on the stove and tossing in a handful of vegetables, seasonings, and meat gives you time to check the anchor and secure the boat for the evening. Then it's time to eat!

For the Basic Soup recipe, you can combine all the dry ingredients in a bag at home. Then all you have to do is dump them into boiling water without taking time to measure.

Basic Soup

4 cups water
4 chicken or beef bouillon cubes
1 tablespoon oil (optional)
$^{1}/_{2}$ pound meat (optional)
1 small tomato, 2 to 3 tablespoons tomato paste, or small handful of sun-dried tomatoes
1 carrot, chopped (freeze-dried is OK)
$^{1}/_{2}$ cup freeze-dried peas
$^{1}/_{2}$ cup freeze-dried potato slices
1 teaspoon celery seeds
2 tablespoons dried parsley
2 tablespoons dried onion flakes
pepper to taste
garlic powder to taste

In pot over medium flame, heat oil and brown meat. Do not burn. Add water and bouillon cubes. Bring to a boil and add all other ingredients. Reduce heat and cover. Simmer for about 25 to 30 minutes.

Fast Pea Soup

3 cups water
$1/4$ teaspoon salt (optional)
1 cup freeze-dried peas (more for thicker soup)
$1/2$ cup ham, diced
2 carrots, diced
1 teaspoon thyme

In pot over medium flame, bring salted water to boil. Add all ingredients and cover. Simmer for about 45 minutes or longer to cook down peas, stirring occasionally. Serve with soda crackers or bread.

This next soup was inspired by those hardy souls who paddled the North Country in search of furs during the 18th and 19th centuries. It takes a long time to cook, so keep it for a layover day when there's a cold rain, the wind is blowing, and a little extra heat in the cabin will be welcome.

Voyageur Pea Soup

4 cups water (or more)
2 cups dried (not freeze-dried) yellow or green peas
1 large onion, diced
1 large carrot, peeled and diced
$1/2$ cup ham, diced
salt and pepper to taste
1 to 2 tablespoons flour

Soak dried peas in water for about 6 hours (or overnight). When ready to cook, add water to bring to 2 cups. Add salt (if desired) and bring to boil over medium flame, stirring to prevent sticking. Add ham, carrot, and onion. Cover and reduce heat. Cook for at least 1 hour, adding flour to thicken if desired.

Sometimes, familiar territory tastes best when your stomach asks if the soup's on. This one's also a good bet when you're waiting out a passing cold front.

Sailor's Penicillin

2 chicken legs, disjointed

5 cups water

1 teaspoon salt (optional)

4 carrots, diced

2 tablespoons onion flakes

pepper to taste

2 bay leaves

$^1/_2$ teaspoon thyme

1 cup uncooked noodles

In pot over medium flame, bring salted water to gentle boil. Cook chicken until meat falls off bone (about 45 minutes), adding water as needed. Remove meat and bones from broth. Discard bones and cut meat into small pieces. Add all other ingredients except noodles. Cook another 25 minutes or until carrots are done. Add noodles and cook until tender.

The powers of chicken soup are legendary. For Don, the ultimate chicken soup has to be a major meal in a bowl. And that means chicken stew.

Souper Cluck Stew

1 tablespoon vegetable oil

2 chicken breasts (or softpack), cut in chunks

4 cups water (or more)

4 chicken bouillon cubes

4 potatoes, peeled and diced

2 carrots, chopped

2 medium onions, chopped

$^1/_2$ teaspoon cayenne pepper

2 cloves garlic, crushed

$^1/_2$ teaspoon pepper

1 large tomato, in chunks
1 15-ounce can corn, drained
flour

Heat oil in pan. Brown chicken in oil (avoid burning). Place all other ingredients except corn and tomato in pot over medium-high heat. Bring to boil, cover, and reduce heat. Simmer 30 minutes. Add corn and tomato, and simmer another 15 minutes. Add water as needed. Thicken with flour as needed.

Chow-Hound Chowder

1 tablespoon vegetable oil
2 chicken breasts (or softpack), chopped
3 cups water
1 15-ounce can corn, drained
1 large onion, chopped
2 stalks celery, chopped
1 packet dried nonfat milk (1-quart size, or $1\frac{1}{3}$ cups)
2 to 3 tablespoons flour
salt and pepper to taste

In pot, heat oil and sauté chicken until cooked through. Then add remaining ingredients except flour. Heat over medium flame. If thickening is needed, mix flour with a few table-spoons of water to make a paste. Stir well while adding this to stew to prevent lumps.

Instead of "cluck," you might want "moo" in your meal. If so, take a shot at a high-powered soup that's got more mulligan in it than a 6:45 a.m. Saturday tee time.

Big-Time Beef Stew

$^1/_2$ pound stew beef, cut in 1-inch cubes

1 cup flour

2 to 3 tablespoons vegetable oil

2 cups water

2 medium potatoes, cubed (leave skin on)

1 medium onion, cut in chunks

2 carrots, cut in chunks

salt and pepper to taste

1 bay leaf

1 teaspoon Worcestershire sauce

celery seed to taste

1 egg, beaten

Place flour in bowl and dredge meat in flour. Over medium flame, heat pot and add oil. Brown floured meat, turning to prevent sticking. Save leftover flour. Add water to pot, scraping bottom with spoon. Add all other ingredients, cover, and simmer at least 30 minutes. Stir occasionally. Add a little water, a few dashes of vegetable oil, and the beaten egg to remaining flour. Mix into a sticky dough. With oiled spoon, drop balls of dough into stew, cover pan again, and cook 5 more minutes. *Do not stir* stew after you add the dumplings.

This is a hearty soup that uses a beef soup bone and ham hocks. If you won't be at a dock with access to a garbage can, you may want to try a different soup recipe or else you'll end up lugging some heavy food waste around with you.

Long Day Soup

1 beef soup bone
2 ham hocks (about 1½ pounds)
1 teaspoon cayenne pepper
2 cups black-eyed peas (presoak 4 to 5 hours in 2 quarts of cold water)
2 large onions, cut into chunks
1 gallon water

Boil all ingredients over medium-to-medium-high heat for 1 hour until peas are soft. Strip meat from beef bone and ham hocks and reserve. Discard fat, skin, bones. Remove ½ cup of peas from soup and mash with fork. Mix mashed peas into broth. Return meat to soup and simmer for another 30 minutes.

Corn Chowder

1 tablespoon vegetable oil
1 medium onion, diced
1 stalk celery, diced
2 tablespoons flour
1 cup water
1 15-ounce can corn, drained
½ cup low-fat milk (or make from powdered)
salt and pepper to taste

Heat pan over medium flame. Add oil and diced vegetables. Sauté for 2 to 3 minutes. Add the flour and cook (don't let veggies or flour brown!) for another 4 minutes. Add the water, corn, and milk. Bring to a boil over high flame and cook, stirring occasionally. Season with salt and pepper, reduce heat to a low simmer, and cook for another 10 minutes. Add water as needed to achieve desired thickness.

Here's a vegetarian stew from Chris Townsend.

Carrot and Lentil Stew

4 cups water
$^1/_2$ cup lentils
2 large carrots, diced
1 large onion, diced
2 garlic cloves, crushed
1 large tomato, cut into chunks
$^1/_4$ cup fresh parsley, chopped
2 bay leaves
black pepper to taste
chili powder to taste (optional)
pinch of salt

Add all ingredients except salt to 4 cups cold water (more if you prefer a soupy stew), bring to a boil, and then simmer 45 minutes or until lentils are soft. Add salt after cooking (adding it before slows down cooking). Cooking time can be shortened if lentils are presoaked in hot water. Serve with whole-grain bread.

■ VEGETABLES

And speaking of vegetarian dishes, here are a few recipes to make your meals greener and tastier. For a hearty vegetarian pasta dish, try Pasta and Sauce (see page 115) without the beef. Get some extra fiber and even more texture by using whole wheat pasta. For a powerful ratatouille, try the recipe on page 114, substituting mushrooms for the meat. And for other vegetable dishes, turn to the vegetable section in the previous chapter (see pages 61–66) and treat your pot like a pan.

Very Green Stuffed Peppers

1 large onion, $^1/_2$ diced and $^1/_2$ sliced $^1/_4$ inch thick
1 cup precooked wild rice
$^3/_4$ cup precooked Minute Rice
1 large tomato, diced
$^1/_2$ cup seasoned breadcrumbs
1 egg, beaten
6 ounces cheddar cheese, grated
$^1/_4$ cup green olives stuffed with pimentos, chopped
salt and pepper to taste
2 large green peppers
$^1/_2$ to $^3/_4$ cup water

In bowl, mix all ingredients except peppers and onion slices. Cut tops off peppers and clean out seeds. Stuff peppers. Place onion slices on bottom of pot. Place peppers on top of onions. Add water and cover. Over a medium flame, bring water to boil and cook peppers 45 minutes.

The next recipe can work either as a complement to a meal or as a quick stand-alone lunch.

Tasty Pasta with Cheese

2 to 3 quarts water
1 cup uncooked pasta
2 tablespoons olive oil
2 teaspoons vegetable oil
$1/4$ teaspoon hot pepper flakes
salt and pepper to taste
$1/2$ cup shelled walnut pieces or pine nuts
$1/2$ cup grated cheese

Boil salted water in your pot. Add pasta and cook until done. Drain water. Add all other ingredients and gently toss.

————————

Spaghetti with Cheese and Tomato Sauce

2 to 3 quarts water
8 ounces uncooked spaghetti or noodles
1 15-ounce can whole or diced tomatoes, undrained
$1/4$ to $1/4$ cup grated Parmesan or other hard cheese
1 large onion, sliced
1 garlic clove, crushed
1 tablespoon mixed herbs (such as oregano, basil, and fennel seed)
black pepper to taste

Boil water in your pot. Add spaghetti and onion, and cook uncovered for 10 minutes or until spaghetti is cooked, stirring occasionally. Drain water. Add tomatoes, cheese, garlic, and herbs and return to heat, stirring constantly until cheese has melted. You may want to add 1 tablespoon of sugar to sweeten the sauce.

————————

"It's All We Had in the Depression" Tomato Lunch

2$\frac{1}{4}$ cups water
3 large tomatoes
2$\frac{1}{4}$ cups water, divided
1 green pepper, diced
1 onion, diced
2 tablespoons sugar
salt and pepper to taste
$\frac{1}{2}$ cup uncooked Minute Rice

In pot, bring 2 cups water to boil. Scald tomatoes by dipping them in water with slotted spoon for 30 seconds to 1 minute. Remove from water and peel. Discard water. Return tomatoes to pot and add $\frac{1}{4}$ cup water. Cover and cook over low flame for 20 minutes. Add all other ingredients and cook another 10 to 15 minutes, stirring to prevent sticking.

––––––––––

Rib-Stickin' Potato Salad

water
3 large potatoes, peeled and quartered
2 eggs
$\frac{1}{4}$ cup green onion, diced
3 to 4 tablespoons Miracle Whip or mayonnaise
1 tablespoon prepared mustard
salt and pepper to taste
1 cup mushrooms, sliced (optional)

Place potatoes and eggs in pot and add enough water to cover. Boil for 25 minutes. Drain and cut potatoes into small chunks. Peel and dice eggs. Mix with all remaining ingredients in pot.

––––––––––

Here's another from Chris Townsend.

Rice Curry

1 tablespoon vegetable oil

1 cup brown rice

1 large onion, sliced

$1/2$ teaspoon curry powder (or to taste)

2 cups water

1 cup mushrooms, sliced

$1/2$ cup raisins

1 green pepper, chopped

1 large tomato, chopped

1 vegetable bouillon cube

In pot over medium flame, heat oil. Add rice, onion, and curry powder and sauté 1 minute, stirring constantly. Then add $1^1/2$ cups water and the rest of the ingredients. Bring to boil and then simmer, covered, until all the water has been absorbed (about 30 minutes). You can use white rice instead of brown; it cooks in half the time, but the result won't be as tasty or nutritious.

Here's an unusual dish that makes a great cold lunch. Top it off with fruit.

Chilled Sesame Linguine

2 to 3 quarts water

$1/2$ pound thin linguine or spaghetti

1 tablespoon peanut oil

1 teaspoon minced fresh ginger

4 teaspoons sugar

2 tablespoons creamy peanut butter

2 tablespoons soy sauce

1 tablespoon wine vinegar

$1/4$ teaspoon crushed red pepper flakes

2 scallions, cut into 2-inch pieces

Boil water in large pot and cook pasta. Drain and toss with peanut oil; set aside to cool. In small bowl, whisk together remaining ingredients except scallions. Pour over cooled pasta. Before serving, toss well and sprinkle scallions over the top.

———————

One of our favorite recipes is something Don's wife, Pam, picked up while she was taking a course at Northern Illinois University.

Vegetarian Chili

- 1 cup Textured Vegetable Protein (TVP); available at many natural food stores
- $7/8$ cup boiling water
- 1 medium onion, chopped
- 1 teaspoon olive oil
- 1 $14^1/_2$-ounce can whole tomatoes, undrained
- 1 15-ounce can kidney beans, drained
- 1 to 2 cups vegetable broth
- 1 tablespoon chili powder
- 1 teaspoon dried oregano
- $1/_2$ teaspoon cumin powder
- salt to taste

In small bowl, combine boiling water and TVP to rehydrate (takes about 10 minutes). In a heavy pot, sauté onion in oil. Add all the remaining ingredients. Reserve 1 cup of broth, adding as necessary to achieve desired thickness. Simmer uncovered for 15 minutes, stirring occasionally. Serves 4.

———————

■ MEAT

Your pot gives you a chance to experiment with beef in ways you just can't do in a frying pan. The simple fact is that, depending on the cut, beef can be tough and stringy. Cheap cuts cooked in a frying pan can mean tough times when the dinner bell rings.

The pot helps solve that problem. Because you'll be cooking the meat for more than 30 minutes in most cases, you can use chuck or round where you might otherwise want sirloin. The extended cooking time helps tenderize the cheaper cuts, which means you can go easy on your budget while creating a meal that goes easy on your taste buds.

Beef has a stronger flavor than poultry and supports more heady spice combinations. Don't be afraid to experiment. Beef also makes a heartier gravy that presents well against starches like potatoes, noodles, and rice.

Basic Beef in a Pot

$^1/_2$ pound boneless bottom round, cut in strips
3 tablespoons flour
2 tablespoons vegetable oil

Choose one of the following sauces:

Red Sauce

1 green pepper, diced
$^1/_2$ cup water
1 large tomato, crushed
1 teaspoon onion flakes
$^1/_4$ teaspoon paprika
salt and pepper to taste

Cream Sauce

3 large mushrooms, sliced
1 medium potato, thinly sliced
1 cup water
1 cup milk
1 tablespoon flour
pepper to taste

Brown Sauce

    1 carrot, chopped
    1 tablespoon sugar
    1 cup water
    1 tablespoon flour
    1 teaspoon onion flakes
    $^1/_4$ teaspoon garlic powder
    salt and pepper to taste

In a plastic bag, shake beef in flour until coated. In pot over medium flame, heat oil and brown meat, taking care not to burn meat. For the Red Sauce, add green pepper and sauté until tender, adding extra oil if needed. For the Cream Sauce variation, sauté mushrooms and potatoes. For the Brown Sauce recipe, sauté carrots and add sugar to caramelize both the vegetable and the beef.

At this point, add all other ingredients for the selected sauce base. Reduce heat and cover. Cook between 35 and 45 minutes, stirring occasionally to prevent sticking. Add water to keep sauce reduction to a minimum. Serve over noodles, over rice, or with rolls. If you didn't bring precooked noodles or rice, you can add either one to the pot before the final 35- to 45-minute simmering. Just be sure you have enough liquid left to cook the starch—add more if necessary. An uncooked vegetable as a side dish fills out the meal.

No doubt you've figured out that the pot, like the frying pan, is a great way to take a trip around the world. Sort of like taking one cruise and then adding another to it.

Garibaldi's Roast Beef

$^1/_2$ to $^3/_4$ pound rump or round roast

2 teaspoons olive oil

$^1/_2$ teaspoon garlic powder

$^1/_2$ teaspoon basil

2 tablespoons prepared mustard

2 tablespoons olive oil

1 cup water

1 medium green pepper, cut in strips

2 medium potatoes, sliced (leave skin on)

1 medium sweet red pepper, cut in strips

1 large onion, chopped

Rub oil, garlic powder, basil, and mustard on roast. Heat pot over medium flame and add oil. Brown meat on all sides. Add water, cover, and cook about 1 hour. Add vegetables. Cover and cook another 30 minutes. Serve with Italian bread and a nice Sangiovese.

————————

Pedro's Rice

$^1/_2$ pound ground beef

1 large onion, chopped

1 medium green pepper, chopped

5 plum tomatoes, crushed

$1^1/_2$ cups water

$^3/_4$ cup uncooked rice

$^1/_2$ teaspoon chili powder

salt and pepper to taste

In pot over medium flame, brown meat until crumbly and drain grease. Add all other ingredients and stir thoroughly. Bring to moderate boil. Cover, reduce heat, and cook about 20 minutes or until rice is tender.

————————

"Safe" Chili

$1/2$ to $3/4$ pound sirloin, cut in bite-size chunks
1 teaspoon vegetable oil
1 large onion, chopped
1 clove garlic, crushed
1 large tomato, chopped
6 large mushrooms, sliced
1 15-ounce can corn, drained
1 6-ounce can tomato paste
$3/4$ cup water
$1^1/2$ teaspoons chili powder
$1/4$ teaspoon pepper
$1/4$ teaspoon ground cumin
salt to taste

Over medium flame, heat oil in pot and brown meat. Add all other ingredients. Cover and simmer for 15 to 20 minutes or until vegetables are tender.

Ratatouille is usually vegetables only. But beef makes an interesting taste difference. If you want to make it vegetarian, substitute 2 cups of portobello sliced mushrooms for the meat.

Beef Ratatouille

$1/2$ pound round steak, thinly sliced

4 tablespoons olive oil

1 large onion, sliced

1 clove garlic, crushed

1 large green pepper, diced

1 medium-to-large summer squash or zucchini, sliced

1 medium eggplant, diced

1 large tomato, cut in chunks

1 6-ounce can tomato paste

1 cup water

2 to 3 tablespoons sugar

1 bay leaf

$1/4$ teaspoon fennel seed

salt and pepper to taste

Parmesan or Romano cheese (optional)

Heat oil in pot over medium flame. Brown meat, add onion, and sauté until onion is soft. Add all other ingredients. Cover and reduce heat. Stir often. Cook about 35 minutes or until sauce thickens. Add grated Parmesan or Romano cheese.

———————

Here is another version of an old-time favorite.

Meaty Stuffed Peppers

$1/2$ to $3/4$ pound ground beef

1 large onion, $1/2$ diced and $1/2$ sliced $1/4$ inch thick

$2/3$ cup uncooked Minute Rice

1 medium tomato, diced

1 egg, beaten

$1/4$ teaspoon hot pepper sauce

garlic salt and pepper to taste
2 large green peppers
$^1/_2$ cup water

In bowl, mix all ingredients except peppers and onion slices. Cut tops off peppers and remove seeds. Divide stuffing evenly and pack each pepper. Place onion slices on bottom of pot. Place peppers upright in pot on top of onion slices, add water, and cover. Over medium flame, bring water to boil. Cook 45 minutes. Check to keep water level at least 1 inch up on peppers.

———————

Sticking with good ground beef for a moment, here's another super-easy take on a dependable standby.

Pasta and Sauce

$^1/_2$ to $^3/_4$ pound ground beef
1 tablespoon olive oil
1 medium onion, diced
1 clove garlic, crushed
1 medium green pepper, diced
1 large tomato, crushed
1 6-ounce can tomato paste
1 cup water
2 teaspoons oregano
1 teaspoon basil
$^1/_2$ teaspoon fennel seed
$1^1/_2$ tablespoons sugar
2 tablespoons Parmesan cheese
salt and pepper to taste
2 cups precooked pasta (cook very al dente and store in plastic bag)

Over low flame, brown ground beef in pot. Drain and add oil. Heat over medium flame. Add onion, garlic, and green pepper and sauté with meat until tender. Add tomato paste, water, seasonings, sugar, and cheese, stirring to mix evenly. Simmer 25 minutes. Add salt and pepper to taste, then mix in precooked pasta. Add water if blend becomes too dry. Remove from heat and serve with Caesar salad, Chianti, and breadsticks. For a vegetarian sauce, omit the meat.

———————

Beefy, Cheesy Elbows

$^2/_3$ pound ground beef

1 large onion, diced

2 teaspoons vegetable oil

4 ounces cheddar cheese, cut into small cubes

$^1/_2$ cup milk

salt and pepper to taste

4 cups precooked macaroni

Heat pot over medium flame and add oil. Sauté onions and beef until well cooked. Spoon off as much grease as possible. Add cheese, milk, and seasonings. Cover and simmer over low heat until cheese is melted. Add macaroni. Heat for 5 minutes and serve.

A traditional pot recipe comes to us from the farms and chateaus of France.

Drunken Beef

$^3/_4$ pound sirloin, cut in 1-inch chunks

flour

2 tablespoons oil, butter, or margarine

1 large onion, chopped

1 clove garlic, diced

1 package mushroom soup (single-serving size)

1 cup water

salt and pepper to taste

$^1/_2$ cup dry red wine

2 cups precooked noodles

Dredge meat in flour. Heat pot over medium flame and add oil. Brown the beef. Add onion and garlic and sauté until tender. Add all other ingredients. Bring to boil. Reduce heat, cover, and simmer 35 minutes. Serve over precooked noodles.

Other traditions can be found closer to home. You don't need to be from Boston or Brooklyn to enjoy this "broguishly" flavored dish!

Corned Beef à la Michael

> $^3/_4$ pound corned beef, rinsed
> water
> $^1/_2$ head cabbage
> 2 large onions, quartered
> 2 large potatoes, peeled and cut in half
> 4 carrots, cut in chunks
> 1 teaspoon celery flakes
> 2 bay leaves
> pepper to taste

In pot, cover meat with water and simmer about 1 hour, making sure that water does not boil off. Drain water and add all other ingredients. Cover meat and vegetables with fresh water. Bring to gentle boil, reduce heat, and cover. Cook over low flame about 1 hour.

Tick-Tock Minute Steak

> 2 cube steaks (about $^1/_2$ pound total)
> salt and pepper to taste
> garlic powder to taste
> 1 large onion, sliced
> 1 cup uncooked Minute Rice
> 1 cup fresh green beans, chopped
> 1 6-ounce can tomato paste
> 2 cups water

Season meat with salt, pepper, and garlic powder. Layer ingredients in pot: onion, then meat, then rice, then beans. Combine water and tomato paste and pour over everything. Cover and cook over medium heat 30 minutes.

Beef à la MacArthur

$1/4$ pound dried beef (4-ounce jar or bag)
1 cup water
1 cup milk
2 to 3 tablespoons flour
2 hard-boiled eggs, chopped
salt and white pepper to taste

In pot over medium flame, bring meat and water to boil. Cook about 5 minutes. Remove from heat and drain water. This helps reduce the saltiness. Add milk and return to heat. Warm, but *do not boil*. Slowly stir in flour to thicken sauce. Add eggs and season with salt and pepper. Cook no longer than 5 minutes more. Serve over a split hard roll.

The crowning achievement for beef in a pot is just that—the all-American pot roast.

Red, White, and Brown Pot Roast

$1/2$ to $3/4$ pound pot roast (boneless, if possible)
salt and pepper to taste
1 tablespoon vegetable oil
2 cups water
3 beef bouillon cubes
2 large potatoes, peeled and quartered
3 large carrots, sliced
1 or 2 large onions, cut in chunks

Season meat with salt and pepper. Add oil and meat to pot over medium flame and quickly brown meat on all sides. Immediately add remaining ingredients and simmer over medium flame 45 minutes or longer. Stir occasionally to keep from sticking.

Beyond beef are pork and ham. All too often, people complain that pork is too dry. In the pot, it won't be.

Peasant Pork Chops

2 stalks celery, chopped
1 medium onion, cut in chunks
2 carrots, cut in chunks
1 potato, quartered
1 large tomato, crushed
1 turnip, peeled and cut in chunks
$1^1/_2$ cups water
$^1/_2$ teaspoon salt (optional)
1 beef bouillon cube
1 bay leaf
$^1/_4$ teaspoon thyme
pepper to taste
2 center-cut pork loin chops

Combine all vegetables and seasonings with water in pot. Place chops on top. Cook over a medium flame for 1 hour. Stir once after 30 minutes. Make sure that water does not boil away.

Souper Chops

2 center-cut pork loin chops, thick cut
$^2/_3$ cup uncooked Minute Rice
2 cups water
1 can mushroom soup (condensed is best)
1 single-serving packet onion soup mix
$^1/_2$ pound baby carrots

Combine all ingredients in pot, mix well, cover, and bring to boil. Stir to keep rice from sticking, reduce heat, and cook over low heat for 30 minutes. Stir occasionally to prevent burning.

Big Mo Chops

  2 center-cut pork loin chops, thick cut
  1 large onion, sliced
  1 large green pepper, cut in strips
  2 large potatoes, sliced
  2 tablespoons ketchup
  2 tablespoons molasses
  2 tablespoons water

In pot over medium flame, brown chops. Remove from pot and drain fat. Layer ingredients as follows: sliced onion, then meat, then other vegetables. Brush with ketchup and molasses. Drizzle water over top. Cover and cook 40 minutes over low heat. Add additional water if sauce is too thick.

———————

And what about bacon? It isn't just for breakfast anymore.

Belly Bustin' Spuds

  $1/2$ pound bacon, diced
  1 large onion, chopped
  1 large green pepper, chopped
  2 stalks celery, chopped
  2 large potatoes, sliced (we're talking big bakers here!)
  $1/4$ cup fresh parsley, chopped

 In pot over medium flame, cook bacon. Do not drain. Add onions, peppers, and celery. Sauté until tender. Add potatoes, stir, and reduce heat. Stir occasionally. After 30 minutes, add parsley. Cook until potatoes start to fall apart.

———————

PRESSURE-COOKER RECIPES

Rice, beans, and meat all fare well in a pressure cooker. Here are some of our favorites.

Mirro Arroz

> 1 cup white rice
> $2^1/_2$ cups water

Put rice in a stainless steel mixing bowl on the pressure cooker rack. Add $1^1/_2$ cups of water to the rice in the bowl and put 1 cup of water in the bottom of the cooker. Bring to pressure and cook 5 minutes. Then remove cooker from the burner (or just turn off the heat) and let the cooker depressurize itself. When you open the cooker, let the rice sit for another 5 minutes before serving.

☛ *Note: If you are using brown rice, cook for about 17 minutes.*

———————

You can make your rice more interesting by adding spices such as curry, and by cooking meat with the rice. Try canned chicken or tuna, fresh chicken cut into bite-size pieces, ground beef, or cut-up beef or pork. As long as the pieces of meat are small, even fresh meat will cook thoroughly. You could also add tomatoes or tomato paste, etc.

These next few are good for both you and your boat!

Salt Sea Beans

2 cups dried black, navy, or pinto beans
water
$^1/_4$ cup vegetable oil
1 tablespoon salt (optional—see instructions)
$4^1/_4$ cups water (for cooking beans)

Soak beans overnight in water, oil, and salt. If you are at sea and have clean seawater, use it to soak the beans, but omit the salt. Pour the used water into the head (instead of the galley sink); the oil in the water will lubricate the head. Rinse the beans with fresh water, add fresh soaking water, and soak all day. To cook, add $4^1/_4$ cups water, and cook in the pressure cooker following the instructions with your cooker. We love garlic with our beans and add 2 or 3 cloves of crushed garlic before cooking the beans.

Pony Boy Pintos

$^3/_4$ cup pinto beans
$^1/_4$ cup oil
water
1 clove garlic, crushed
1 16-ounce can tomatoes
$1^2/_3$ cups water
1 to 2 tablespoons of oil

Soak overnight in $^1/_4$ cup oil and water, as described above. Rinse beans with fresh water, add fresh soaking water, and soak all day. To cook, place beans in pressure cooker with the rest of the ingredients. Cook for 35 minutes, remove from heat, and let cooker depressurize itself. If you do not use the can of tomatoes, use $2^1/_4$ cups of water.

Heart of Darkness Bean Blast

> $^3/_4$ cup black beans
> water
> $^1/_4$ cup oil
> $2^1/_2$ cups water
> 1 to 2 tablespoons of oil
> $^1/_3$ cup bacon, pork, or ham, diced

Soak beans overnight with water and oil, as described previously. Rinse beans with fresh water, add fresh soaking water, and soak all day. To cook, place in pressure cooker with the rest of the ingredients. Cook 30 minutes, remove from heat, and allow cooker to depressurize itself.

☛ *Tip: You can add $^1/_4$ cup white rice and another $^1/_2$ cup water to cooker to have rice and beans. If you want a smaller portion of beans, use $^2/_3$ cup dried (unsoaked) beans and 2 cups water in the cooker.*

———————

You can also use your pressure cooker to put some fine food on the galley boards. Try these on for size.

"By the Hair of My . . . " Ham Bake

> 1 $1^1/_2$-pound canned ham
> Dijon mustard
> whole cloves
> 1 cup water

Coat ham with mustard, stud with cloves, and place on rack. Add water and cook for 15 minutes. Remove from heat and let cooker depressurize itself.

———————

Susan's Special Meatloaf

1 pound ground beef or turkey

$^{1}/_{2}$ bottle Heinz chili sauce

1 egg

$^{1}/_{2}$ cup old-fashioned oatmeal or breadcrumbs

$^{1}/_{2}$ cup raisins

1 cup water

Mix all ingredients except water together. Put in disposable aluminum loaf pan (one that will fit in your pressure cooker) or in a stainless steel mixing bowl and place on rack. Add water and cook 15 minutes. Remove from heat and let cooker depressurize itself.

Yummy Yams and Pork Chops

2 pork chops, $^{3}/_{4}$ to 1 inch thick

1 tablespoon oil

2 to 3 small to medium yams (sweet potatoes), cut in half

1 cup water

Trim excess fat from pork chops. Heat oil and brown chops in bottom of the cooker. Place chops and yams on rack in cooker and add water. Bring to pressure and cook for 8 minutes with regulator rocking moderately. Let cooker depressurize itself.

☛ *Tip: If you want to use $^{1}/_{2}$-inch-thick chops, cut yams in smaller pieces and cook chops and yams for 5 to 6 minutes.*

Stuffed Peppers under Pressure

$^{1}/_{2}$ pound ground beef or turkey

$^{1}/_{4}$ cup uncooked rice or quinoa

$^{3}/_{8}$ cup ketchup or chili sauce

1 egg

$^{1}/_{4}$ to $^{1}/_{2}$ teaspoon garlic flakes

1 medium onion, chopped

2 large or 3 medium green peppers
1¹/₂ cups water

Mix together everything but the peppers in a bowl. Cut tops off peppers and remove seeds. Divide the meat mixture among the peppers. Put water in cooker and stand stuffed peppers on the rack. (You can also put the peppers in a round cake pan and place the pan on the rack.) Bring to pressure and cook for 10 minutes with the regulator rocking moderately. Let cooker depressurize itself.

DESSERT

Compotes, puddings, baked fruits—all are taste delights sure to top off a great meal. Your pot is the perfect venue for flavor and fun.

Indian Pudding

1 can sweetened condensed milk
¹/₂ cup water
3 tablespoons butter or margarine
3 tablespoons brown sugar
¹/₂ teaspoon nutmeg
¹/₂ teaspoon cinnamon
2 eggs, beaten
¹/₂ to ³/₄ cup cornmeal
¹/₄ cup raisins

In pot over medium flame, bring sweetened condensed milk and water to gentle boil. Reduce heat and add butter, sugar, and spices. Once sugar is dissolved, add eggs, cornmeal, and raisins. Stir. Cover and cook over low flame for 10 minutes. Stir often to keep from sticking.

Orange Pudding

2 oranges, peeled and segmented (or substitute a 6-ounce can of mandarin
orange segments, drained)
1 teaspoon plus 1½ tablespoons sugar
²/₃ cup milk
1 egg yolk (reserve egg white for topping)
salt (optional)
1 teaspoon cornstarch

Topping

1 egg white
½ teaspoon sugar

For pudding, sprinkle 1 teaspoon sugar over oranges in bowl. In double boiler over medium flame, combine milk, egg yolk, a pinch of salt, cornstarch, and 1½ tablespoons sugar. Stir until mixture thickens. Pour over oranges. Allow to cool. If you wish a topping, whip egg white until stiff, fold in sugar, and spoon onto pudding.

Here's a favorite of a British friend of Don's.

Trifle

³/₄ cup fresh strawberries, sliced (or use blueberries)
sugar
2 Twinkies, sliced the long way

Custard

1 cup milk
2 egg yolks, beaten (reserve egg whites for topping)
2 tablespoons sugar
1 teaspoon cornstarch

Topping

2 egg whites
1 teaspoon sugar

Put berries in a bowl, sprinkle with sugar, and place the Twinkies on top. To make custard, combine milk, egg yolks, sugar, and cornstarch in a double boiler over medium flame. Stir until mixture thickens. Pour over fruit and Twinkies. Allow to cool. If you wish a topping, beat egg whites until stiff, fold in sugar, and spoon onto trifle.

This unusual combination tastes great after a long day.

Mac's Surprise

$^1/_2$ cup uncooked white rice

1 cup water

$^1/_2$ cup raisins

1 apple, peeled, cored, and sliced

1 tablespoon brown sugar

$^1/_2$ teaspoon cinnamon

$^1/_4$ teaspoon nutmeg

1 tablespoon powdered nonfat milk

In pot over medium flame, combine rice and water and bring to boil. Add raisins and apple. Stir. Cover and cook until rice is tender, about 15 minutes. Remove from flame and add all other ingredients. Stir and let cool for 10 minutes. If you wish, add a little more milk and sugar.

Earlier, we talked about steaming vegetables. Well, you can do the same with fruit.

Apple Delight

2 McIntosh apples, top halves peeled

2 tablespoons raisins

1 tablespoon sugar

cinnamon to taste

water

Core apples without puncturing bottoms. In bowl, mix sugar and raisins. Stuff each apple with raisin-sugar mixture. Sprinkle cinnamon over top. Pour enough water in pot to reach bottom of steamer. Place apples on steamer. Cover pot and place over medium flame. Allow to steam at least 30 minutes, adding water if needed.

Pears 'n' Cots

Same recipe as previous, except substitute fresh pears for apples, diced dried apricots for raisins, and fresh mint leaves (finely diced) for cinnamon.

———————

Creativity is the rule for desserts in a pot. You can stew or cook just about any fruit to make applesauce, "pearsauce," or fruit compote quickly and easily. Just chop the basic ingredients, add various spices to taste, and throw in molasses, brown sugar, or white sugar, depending on how you want the dish to look and taste.

Fruit Compote

$\frac{1}{2}$ cup dried apricots

$\frac{1}{2}$ cup raisins

1 6-ounce can mandarin orange slices, drained

1 fresh peach, peeled and cored

3 tablespoons sugar

$\frac{1}{3}$ cup water

In pot over medium flame, combine all ingredients. Cover and cook at least 20 minutes. Stir often and add more water as needed. Sauce should be thick. Serve with sponge cake or fancy cookies.

———————

Spiced Applesauce

3 large Granny Smith apples, peeled, cored, and cut in chunks

$\frac{1}{2}$ cup water

2 tablespoons brown sugar

$\frac{1}{2}$ teaspoon cinnamon

$\frac{1}{4}$ teaspoon nutmeg

In pot over medium flame, cook apples in water until they fall apart. Remove from heat and stir to make sauce. Add sugar and spices. Tastes great with oatmeal cookies, or serve with or over oatmeal for breakfast!

———————

the
Oven

As Monty Python would say, "And now for something completely different." For any cruising chef, the height of adventurous cooking can be found in all those things that aren't the pot or the pan. In other words, you can challenge your culinary skills and your taste buds by expanding your cooking horizons to include an oven. Even something as basic as the stovetop "ovens" described in the Cruising Galley chapter can turn out casseroles, roasts, and baked goodies in good order. They will also keep you on your toes, making sure that what you're cooking gets roasted or baked, not burned to a crisp.

The recipes in this chapter will work equally well in any sort of oven, built-in or stovetop. If you're using a pressure cooker for your stovetop oven, you may need to spray the inside of the cooker or your "baking dish" with nonstick cooking spray (which isn't needed with the Outback Oven because its pan has a nonstick coating).

Unless otherwise indicated, all cooking temperatures should be in a "medium" oven of 325 to 350°F, or in the middle of the Bake scale on the Outback Oven's thermometer. The pressure-cooker oven cooks at a lower temperature, so you'll need to add a few minutes to the baking time.

Speaking of ovens, a lot of marine cooking is done right on a dock or a beach using a grill. If you read the manuals that come with these versatile pieces of hardware, you'll discover that almost all manufacturers offer accessories that allow you to take full advantage of their equipment for baking. These racks and pans are excellent investments and will help you vary your BBQ fare with steamed (corn on the cob in the husk), baked (mesquite-smoked turkey breast), and roasted (a few squabs, milord?) dishes. Just about any oven recipe presented here can be turned out quite nicely on a grill.

BREAKFAST

Breakfast from the oven is a bit un-American because the national tendency is to eat breakfasts cooked on the top of the stove. But there are some very satisfying ways to kick off the morning using your oven.

Don's an egg person, so he goes for the yolk rather than the straight line.

Françoise's Quiche

1 prepared pie crust
$1/2$ cup cheddar cheese, diced
$1/2$ cup ham, diced
$1/2$ cup evaporated milk
4 eggs
salt and pepper to taste

Line a 9-inch pie plate with pie crust and cut off excess. Crimp edges of crust. Spread cheese on bottom and add ham on top of cheese. Beat milk, eggs, and salt and pepper together and pour over ham and cheese. In a medium oven, cook for 15 to 20 minutes or until filling is firm and top is browned.

Oniony Quiche

Same as previous recipe, but substitute sliced Bermuda onions for ham and use either Swiss or jack cheese.

(Don't) Bern th' Eggs!

1 tablespoon butter or margarine
$1/3$ cup Swiss cheese, grated
$1/4$ cup evaporated milk
2 eggs

Warm oven pan over stove and melt butter. Sprinkle about three-fourths of the cheese on bottom of pan. Break eggs onto the cheese without breaking yolks. Pour milk over and sprinkle with remaining cheese. Place in medium oven for 20 minutes. Serve with hard roll and fresh fruit. Serves 1.

McIntosh Surprise

2 medium McIntosh apples
1/3 pound sausage
2 eggs
salt and pepper to taste

Core apples from the top, but don't break through bottom. Using a spoon, hollow out inside of apple to make a little pocket, widening opening at top. Fill about two-thirds full with sausage. Place in small baking pan. Break an egg on top of the sausage (sides of apple will hold it in place). Bake in medium oven at least 25 to 30 minutes. Add salt and pepper to taste.

Your eyes will remember this recipe immediately. The odor of onions on your hands will remind you of it all day.

Bermuda Eggs

1 medium Bermuda onion
2 large eggs
1 tablespoon Parmesan cheese
1/4 teaspoon tarragon
2 tablespoons parsley, chopped
2 tablespoons breadcrumbs
pepper to taste

Cut onion in half along "equator" (stem and root ends being the poles). Scoop out inner rings of onion, leaving two "cups." Place onion halves in oven pan and break an egg into each. Dice remaining onion and sprinkle on eggs. Combine cheese, tarragon, parsley, breadcrumbs, and pepper. Place healthy scoop on top of each onion. Gently smooth to cover. Add extra as needed. Cook in medium oven for about 15 minutes or until breadcrumbs are browned. For added flavor, sprinkle with diced ham before cooking. Serves 1 (if you're a 2-egger) or 2.

You can also use your oven to build some truly remarkable creations.

Amsterdam Apple Pancake

> 2 tablespoons butter or margarine
> 4 tablespoons brown sugar
> 2 large apples, peeled, cored, and sliced lengthwise about $1/4$ inch thick
> $1/2$ teaspoon cinnamon
> 2 eggs, beaten
> $1/2$ cup milk
> $2/3$ cup Bisquick

In 9-inch round cake pan, melt butter and spread brown sugar evenly on bottom of pan. Layer apple slices on sugar. Sprinkle with cinnamon. Combine egg, milk, and Bisquick and pour batter over fruit and sugar. Bake about 20 minutes in medium oven or until top of pancake is nicely browned. Flip onto plate so brown sugar and apples are on top.

Ed's German Pancake

> nonstick cooking spray
> 4 tablespoons brown sugar
> 2 large apples—peeled, cored, and sliced lengthwise about $1/4$ inch thick
> $1/2$ teaspoon cinnamon
> 2 eggs, beaten
> $1/2$ cup milk
> $2/3$ cup Bisquick

Combine eggs, milk, and Bisquick. Spray 9-inch round cake pan and pour in half of batter. In another bowl, combine apples, brown sugar, and cinnamon. Gently place fruit on top of batter in pan, leaving about 1 inch around edges clear of fruit. Pour remaining batter on top of fruit. Bake about 20 to 30 minutes in medium oven or until top of pancake is nicely browned.

Rasher Cake

2 eggs, separated
$^1/_2$ cup milk
$^1/_2$ teaspoon sugar
$^1/_2$ cup flour
$^1/_2$ cup white cornmeal
1 teaspoon baking powder
6 strips bacon
pepper to taste

Beat egg yolks until light. Add remaining ingredients except bacon and egg whites. Beat egg whites until stiff. Fold into batter. Fry bacon in pan until crisp and drain grease. Transfer bacon to baking pan, pour batter over, and bake in hot (400°F) oven 10 minutes. Reduce heat to 325°F and continue baking until cake is set in center.

LUNCH & DINNER

The oven offers countless opportunities to put variety into your menu from roasts, cakes, and casseroles to pies, bread, snacks, and even pizza. As far as we're concerned, the oven is the best thing going when it's dinnertime.

■ POULTRY

Chicken is one of the easiest meats to cook in the oven, but it can also be one of the most boring. So we'll start with the basics and spice it up from there.

☞ *Note: As mentioned before, when we call for two chicken breasts, we really mean one whole breast (which looks something like a valentine heart) cut in half. Each piece weighs 4 to 6 ounces.*

BBC (Basic Baked Chicken)

$1/2$ pound chicken (white or dark pieces) with skin

1 large onion, sliced

1 stalk celery, chopped

2 or 3 carrots, cut in strips

2 medium potatoes, cut in chunks

salt and pepper to taste

Place chicken in baking pan and surround with vegetables. Add salt and pepper. Bake about 45 minutes in medium oven. Serve with a hard roll and fruit.

'Cued Bird

$^1/_2$ cup hot water

1 beef bouillon cube

1 fresh tomato, crushed

1 tablespoon Worcestershire sauce

4 tablespoons ketchup

1 onion, diced

$^1/_4$ teaspoon dry mustard

1 teaspoon minced fresh parsley

$^1/_4$ teaspoon salt (optional)

$^1/_4$ teaspoon pepper

$^1/_2$ pound chicken (white or dark pieces)

1 cup precooked rice

Dissolve bouillon cube in hot water. Combine with all other ingredients except chicken and rice to make BBQ sauce. Place chicken in oven pan and pour sauce over chicken. Bake 45 minutes in a medium oven. Add precooked rice to pan 10 minutes before removing pan from oven.

————————

Uncle Ben's Chicken

2 boneless, skinless chicken breasts

1 cup seasoned bread stuffing

$^1/_2$ cup water

1 cup precooked long-grain and wild-rice mixture

1 red pepper, cut in strips

1 green pepper, cut in strips

1 carrot, cut in strips

Mix stuffing and water. Flatten chicken breasts slightly (place between wax paper or foil and press with flat side of a knife) and spoon about half the stuffing onto breasts. Roll and secure with toothpick. Place chicken rolls in oven pan. Surround with precooked rice mixture. Dress with pepper and carrot over top. Cover with foil and bake 35 to 45 minutes in medium oven.

————————

This next recipe calls for boneless chicken breasts with the skin still on. Most prepackaged boneless chicken breasts are also skinless, so you can't just run to the local supermarket and buy them. If you aren't lucky enough to have a butcher available to bone your chicken, buy regular chicken breasts and bone them yourself.

Start by turning the meat bone-side up. Assuming that the piece has part of the breast bone still attached, separate the meat from the edge of the bone with a small paring or boning knife. Turn the piece over and slide the blade between the ribs and the meat, cutting the meat away from the breast bone. You should, with practice, be able to bone a chicken breast without losing too much meat.

"Pardon Me, but Do You Have Any . . . " Chicken

2 boneless chicken breasts (leave skin on)
1 clove garlic, minced
2 tablespoons Dijon mustard
$\frac{1}{4}$ teaspoon thyme
salt and pepper to taste

Mix garlic with mustard, thyme, salt, and pepper. Lift up skin gently from meat and rub mixture on chicken. Replace skin and add some more salt and pepper. Place chicken in oven pan and bake 35 to 40 minutes at 350°F.

Great Flavored Bird

2 boneless, skinless chicken breasts
1 fresh lemon
1 tablespoon dried mustard
2 teaspoons brown sugar
$1/2$ teaspoon pepper
$1/2$ teaspoon coriander
2 teaspoons vegetable oil
$3/4$ cup raisins
1 cup precooked noodles

Squeeze lemon and grate about 1 tablespoon of lemon zest (that's the outside of the peel). Combine juice, zest, and dry ingredients. Oil baking pan and place chicken in pan. Bake chicken for 15 minutes in medium to high oven (375°F). Brush with sauce mixture, turn in pan, and bake another 15 minutes. Add raisins and remaining sauce. Bake 15 minutes. Serve with noodles.

Up to this point, we've worked with basic variations on baked chicken. Now let's step up our creativity a notch.

Unusual Bird

2 precooked chicken breasts, diced (or softpack)
2 tablespoons Crisco shortening
$1/3$ cup flour
$1^1/2$ cups milk
2 eggs, beaten
1 cup precooked rice
$1/2$ cup cheddar cheese, grated
salt and pepper to taste

In baking dish on stove, melt Crisco and stir in flour, salt, and pepper. Gradually add milk, stirring to keep from burning. Bring to boil. Remove from heat and add eggs. Stir with whisk until well blended. Stir in chicken. Cover with rice and then cheese. Bake in medium oven 20 minutes.

Crumby Chicken

$^{1}/_{4}$ cup milk

$^{1}/_{2}$ cup seasoned breadcrumbs

$^{1}/_{4}$ cup Parmesan cheese

$^{1}/_{2}$ pound chicken (white or dark pieces)

1 yellow squash or zucchini, cut in 1-inch slices

Mix cheese and breadcrumbs. Dip chicken in milk and roll in coating mix. Place in baking pan. Dip squash in milk and then in coating mix. Arrange vegetables on top of chicken. Bake in medium oven 45 minutes.

———————

Big King Chicken Casserole

2 tablespoons butter or margarine

$^{1}/_{4}$ cup green pepper, diced

1 medium onion, diced

$^{1}/_{2}$ cup mushrooms, sliced

$^{1}/_{4}$ cup flour

1 cup milk

2 eggs, beaten

1 tablespoon bottled or fresh pimiento pepper, thinly sliced

pepper to taste

2 precooked chicken breasts, diced (or softpack)

breadcrumbs

In oven pan on stove, melt butter over medium heat (do not burn). Sauté green pepper, onions, and mushrooms. Add flour and blend. Add milk, egg, pimiento, and pepper. Cook until thick, stirring constantly. Add chicken. Stir and remove from heat. Cover with layer of breadcrumbs and bake 25 minutes or until crust is brown.

———————

Poulet Pie

$^1/_2$ pound precooked chicken, diced (or softpack)

1 packet powdered chicken gravy mix and 1 cup water to prepare

2 prepared pie crusts

2 carrots, diced

1 large potato, thinly sliced

2 stalks celery, diced

Prepare gravy mix in a metal cup over a medium to low flame. Line pie plate with one pie crust. Mix chicken, vegetables, and gravy (you can substitute 1 15-ounce can of chicken gravy for powdered mix and water) and put in pan. Cover with other crust, pinching edges to seal. Cut slits in top crust to vent. Bake in medium oven 45 minutes or until pie crust is nicely browned.

Cheesy Chicken

$^1/_2$ cup Monterey Jack cheese, grated

$^1/_2$ cup milk

$^1/_2$ pound precooked chicken breast, diced (or softpack)

1 cup precooked macaroni

1 sweet red pepper, diced

seasoned breadcrumbs

On stove top over medium flame, heat milk to almost boiling in oven pan or casserole. Slowly add cheese and stir until smooth. Mix in chicken, macaroni, and red pepper. Sprinkle with breadcrumbs. Bake in a medium oven 25 minutes.

Hula Bird

2 boneless, skinless chicken breasts
1 cup fresh or frozen green beans
1 orange, peeled and segmented
1 8-ounce can crushed pineapple
$1/2$ teaspoon ginger
$1/2$ teaspoon cinnamon
1 cup precooked rice

Place chicken breasts in 9-inch round cake pan. Surround with beans. Place orange segments over top and pour pineapple (including juice) over all. Sprinkle with cinnamon and ginger. Cover with foil (not needed with Outback Oven). Bake 45 minutes in medium to high oven. If there's room in pan, add rice 5 minutes before serving. If not, remove chicken from oven at proper time. Wrap rice in foil and heat on top rack for 5 minutes.

———————————

Divine Chicken

2 boneless, skinless chicken breasts
$1^{1}/_{2}$ cups broccoli florets
1 can condensed mushroom soup (do not add water or milk)
breadcrumbs

Line baking pan with foil. Place chicken in pan and cover with broccoli. Pour mushroom soup over all. Sprinkle with breadcrumbs. Cover and bake in medium oven 35 to 40 minutes. To crisp top, uncover last 5 to 10 minutes.

———————————

THE OVEN • LUNCH & DINNER

Paella is the national dish of Spain. This succulent combination of meat, rice, vegetables, and broth starts out on top of the stove and finishes up in the oven. The chef at Café Ba Ba Reeba in Chicago showed Don a great Paella de Verduras (vegetable paella). The following is a meat-enhanced version of that recipe. Use the dark meat from a chicken or turkey because the white meat will dry out during cooking. You can also use pork shoulder, which is moister than a tenderloin cut.

Square-Meal Paella

$^1/_2$ to $^3/_4$ pound boneless chicken thigh meat, diced

3 tablespoons olive oil

1 pound mixed fresh vegetables (beans, cauliflower, broccoli, summer squash, etc.)

1 teaspoon paprika

1 teaspoon garlic, minced

1 large tomato, pureed (about 3 ounces; puree in blender or food processor)

20 ounces chicken broth

2 threads saffron

10 ounces uncooked Spanish rice (if you use arborio, rinse with cold water before cooking to remove some of the starch)

Preheat oven to 450°F. On stove top, in a paella pan (you can use a 12-inch sauté pan), heat oil and brown meat over high heat, stirring frequently. Add the vegetables and sauté until tender. Stir in paprika, garlic, and tomato puree. Add saffron, broth, and rice. Stir and bring to boil. Place uncovered pan in hot oven and cook for 17 to 18 minutes. Remove from oven and let rest 2 or 3 minutes to allow remaining liquids to absorb.

☛ *Note: You can also finish the paella in a kettle-style BBQ using the indirect-heat method. Push the coals to the side of the grill kettle. Place the pan on the grill above the cleared area. Cover the kettle with the lid and cook as above.*

And here's a seafood version.

Chesapeake Paella

³/₄ cup precooked crabmeat, chunk or shredded (you can use imitation in a pinch)

¹/₂ cup bay (small) scallops

3 tablespoons olive oil

1 teaspoon minced garlic

1 teaspoon paprika

¹/₂ cup tomato puree

20 ounces fish broth (you can use chicken broth, but flavor will change)

2 threads saffron

10 ounces uncooked Spanish rice (if you use arborio, rinse with cold water before cooking to remove some of the starch)

1 teaspoon kosher salt

Preheat oven to 450°F. On stove top, in a paella pan (you can use a 12-inch sauté pan), heat oil and sauté crabmeat and scallops for about 2 minutes. Stir in paprika, garlic, and tomato puree. Add saffron, broth, and rice. Stir frequently while bringing to a boil. Taste and add salt if needed. Place uncovered pan in hot oven and cook for 18 to 20 minutes. Remove from oven and let rest 2 or 3 minutes to allow remaining liquids to absorb.

☛ *Note: You can also cook in a covered, hot grill (see previous recipe). Again, cook for 18 to 20 minutes, until liquid is absorbed.*

■ VEGETARIAN DELIGHTS

A lot of these recipes can be considered side dishes, snacks, or à la carte fare. But you can make a full meal out of each one if you take the time to think about the four food groups. You can cover a lot of grain with a kaiser roll and a considerable amount of dairy protein with ½ cup of cheese. So try making one or more of these a centerpiece in your one-pan feast!

If you're using a stovetop oven, this next recipe works best in the Outback Oven because its wide, flat design makes it easy to get the pizza out of the pan. You also could try it in a pressure-cooker oven by putting the pizza dough into a round cake pan, running the dough up the sides of the pan to make your own version of a Chicago-style (deep dish) pizza, and putting that into your "oven." When your pizza is finished baking, serve it from the cake pan.

The One-Pan Pizza

> 1 package pizza dough mix
> 1 tablespoon olive oil
> 1 large tomato, chopped or sliced razor-thin
> ¼ cup mushrooms, sliced
> salt to taste
> ½ teaspoon oregano
> ½ teaspoon minced fresh basil
> ½ cup mozzarella cheese, grated

Prepare dough according to package directions. Flatten dough into a 10-inch circle. Rub with olive oil. Place in bottom pan of your Outback Oven or in your cake pan. (If you're using a traditional oven, place dough on a pizza stone or cookie sheet.) Sprinkle dough with tomato (go for total coverage) and then add mushrooms. Sprinkle with salt and spices and top with the cheese. (If you want to placate a meat lover, add small chunks of precooked sausage or thinly sliced pepperoni before you put on the cheese.) Bake in very hot oven for about 10 to 15 minutes.

John Barley Cake

$^1\!/_2$ cup Bisquick
$1^1\!/_4$ cups water
$^1\!/_2$ cup uncooked barley
1 medium onion, diced
1 medium zucchini, diced
$^1\!/_2$ tablespoon vegetable oil
$^1\!/_4$ teaspoon salt (optional)
$^1\!/_4$ teaspoon oregano

Mix Bisquick with $^3\!/_4$ cup water and stir to remove lumps. Combine with remaining ingredients (including remaining $^1\!/_2$ cup water) in greased pie plate. Cook in medium oven 30 minutes or until water is absorbed and top is firm.

———————

You can try this to add a special touch to your table. (This really doesn't work in an Outback Oven. There just isn't enough headroom for a rising soufflé.)

A-Maize-ing Soufflé

1 tablespoon butter or margarine, at room temperature
1 tablespoon flour
$^3\!/_4$ cup fresh corn
2 eggs, separated
1 cup hot milk
1 teaspoon salt (optional)
pepper and paprika to taste

Blend butter and flour with a fork. To this, add corn, milk, salt, pepper, and paprika. Beat egg yolks until light and add to mixture. Beat egg whites until stiff and fold into mixture. Pour into 6-inch soufflé dish and cook in medium-hot oven about 1 hour.

———————

From this delicate taste treat, you could go all-American—or at least all-Wisconsin.

Macaroni and Cheese Mom's Way

    1 cup milk
    1^1/$_2$ cups Monterey Jack cheese, grated
    3 cups precooked macaroni
    ^{1}/$_2$ cup seasoned breadcrumbs

On medium setting, heat the milk until it almost boils. Gradually add ^{3}/$_4$ cup cheese, stirring so it doesn't burn. When sauce is ready, pour over macaroni in oven pan. Sprinkle with remaining cheese and then with breadcrumbs. Cook in medium oven 25 to 30 minutes or until breadcrumbs are toasty brown.

No-Noodle Lasagna

    1 medium eggplant, cut in ^{1}/$_4$-inch slices (about 10 to 12 slices)
    salt to taste
    1 or 2 eggs
    ^{1}/$_2$ cup milk
    ^{1}/$_2$ cup olive oil
    ^{1}/$_2$ cup seasoned breadcrumbs
    2 cups spaghetti sauce
    8 ounces provolone cheese, sliced

Sprinkle sliced eggplant with salt (if desired) and set aside on towel to drain for 10 minutes. Then rinse. Beat egg(s) with milk. Heat oil in baking pan on stove top on medium setting. Dip eggplant in egg mixture and then into breadcrumbs (both sides). Brown both sides in hot oil. Set on towel to drain. Remove oil from pan and wipe clean. Alternate layers of eggplant, sauce, and cheese in pan, repeating until ingredients are used up. Bake in medium oven 25 to 30 minutes.

Cheesy Spuds

  4 medium potatoes, thinly sliced
  1 large onion, thinly sliced
  6 ounces ham, diced (optional)
  $^1/_2$ cup cheddar cheese, grated
  $^3/_4$ cup milk
  2 tablespoons flour
  salt and pepper to taste

Place potatoes in casserole dish and add layers of ham, cheese, and onion. Whisk together milk, flour, salt, and pepper. Pour over mixture in pan. Bake in medium oven 45 minutes. Sprinkle breadcrumbs on top if you wish.

———————

Peppers à la Shroom

  2 medium green peppers
  $^3/_4$ cup mushrooms, sliced
  1 medium tomato, chopped
  $^1/_2$ cup mozzarella cheese, grated
  $^1/_2$ teaspoon oregano
  $^1/_4$ teaspoon fennel seed
  breadcrumbs

Cut tops off peppers and clean out seeds. Combine mushrooms, tomato, cheese, oregano, and fennel. Stuff peppers. (You can add $^1/_2$ cup precooked rice to stuffing if desired.) Sprinkle breadcrumbs over the top and cook in medium oven 30 to 45 minutes.

———————

Sticking with stuffed vegetables for a moment . . .

Full-House Mushrooms

4 to 6 very large mushrooms
1 small onion, minced
$1/4$ cup fresh spinach leaves, minced
2 teaspoons olive oil
$1/2$ teaspoon basil
$1/4$ teaspoon salt (optional)
$1/4$ teaspoon pepper
1 tablespoon Parmesan cheese
2 tablespoons breadcrumbs

Remove stems from mushrooms. Mince them and combine with remaining ingredients. If mixture doesn't stick together, add more breadcrumbs. Press stuffing firmly into each mushroom cap, mounding stuffing $1/2$ inch or so above edge of cap. Place in oven pan and bake in hot oven (400°F) 10 minutes or until stuffing begins to brown.

Art-I-Choke on These Tomatoes?

1 large tomato
2 marinated artichoke hearts
1 teaspoon olive oil
3 tablespoons seasoned breadcrumbs
2 thick slices provolone cheese
2 jumbo green olives stuffed with pimento

Cut tomato in half. Out of each half, scoop a hole just large enough to hold an artichoke heart. Insert a heart into each tomato half. Mix oil with breadcrumbs and press a handful on top of each tomato half. Bake in medium oven 20 minutes. Lay slice of cheese on top and complete with olive on top of that. Bake another 5 minutes or until cheese melts (but does not run or burn).

---

*Packed with protein, calcium, B vitamins, and fiber, this meal will keep you full
for hours. The beans and rice provide protein complementation, and the cheese
and cottage cheese supply additional protein.*

Cheesy Beans and Rice

1¹/₂ cups precooked brown rice
¹/₂ can (7¹/₂ ounces) kidney beans, drained and repackaged
1 clove garlic, minced
1 medium onion, chopped
1 4-ounce can chopped green chili peppers
4 ounces jack cheese, grated
1 cup low-fat cottage cheese
¹/₂ cup (2 ounces) sharp cheddar cheese, grated

In bowl, combine rice, beans, garlic, onion, and chili peppers. Layer this mixture alternately with the jack cheese and the cottage cheese in an oiled pan. End with a layer of the bean-rice mixture. Bake in medium oven 30 minutes. During the last few minutes of baking, sprinkle the cheddar cheese on top.

Here's a great lunch recipe to serve hot or cold. Don likes to make it ahead of time and serve it cold with a fruit salad. This recipe is very high in protein, iron, calcium, vitamin A, and beta-carotene. It is also relatively low in fat because there is no pie crust. If you don't like spinach, you can substitute broccoli.

Crustless Spinach Pie

1 10-ounce package frozen chopped spinach or broccoli, thawed and well drained
(or use fresh spinach or broccoli, cooked, well drained, and chopped)
$^1/_2$ pound sharp cheddar or feta cheese, grated or crumbled
2 cups low-fat cottage cheese
4 eggs
6 tablespoons flour
$^1/_4$ teaspoon salt
$^1/_2$ teaspoon pepper

In a bowl, combine spinach, grated cheese, and cottage cheese. In a cup, mix eggs with a fork and add flour, salt, and pepper. Combine both mixtures and mix well. Place mixture in a lightly oiled or nonstick-sprayed pie pan, and bake 1 hour in medium oven.

———————

Of course, you can also use your oven simply to bake vegetables.

Solid Squash Surprise

1 acorn squash (1 to 1$^1/_2$ pounds)
1 orange, peeled and halved
2 tablespoons brown sugar
2 tablespoons butter or margarine

Cut squash in half along the equator. Clean out seeds. Trim ends so that the halves do not roll onto their sides. Push half of orange into each cavity, enlarging the cavity as needed. Divide sugar and butter evenly and place on top of orange. Cover with foil. Place on cookie sheet or directly on rack. Bake in hot oven 40 minutes or until squash is tender.

☛ *Note: You can also cook this on the upper rack of a propane or charcoal BBQ (refer to your grill manufacturer's instructions).*

———————

■ BEEF

Here's where the oven can make a big difference in a sailor's life. The world of roasts, of exciting combinations of richly flavored meats and interesting sauces, will come to life as you light up your life and your oven.

The variety of available cuts make beef a versatile choice. Whether you decide to use hamburger or steak, there's always something fun to cook. Remember, though, that beef can be fatty, gristly, tough, or a combination thereof. Cooks, both famous and mundane, have found ways to turn inexpensive beef into toothsome meals fit for lord and lady.

Shepherd's Pie

2 cups instant mashed potatoes, prepared according to package directions
$3/4$ pound lean ground beef (try 95 percent)
salt and pepper to taste
$1/4$ cup flour
$1/4$ cup water
2 to 3 carrots, chopped
1 stalk celery, chopped
1 large onion, chopped

Using your baking pan as a frying pan, brown hamburger over medium heat until crumbly. Reduce heat and add salt, pepper, flour, and water. Stir to make gravy. Remove from heat. Add vegetables and stir to mix. Make crust of prepared mashed potatoes over the top of the meat-and-vegetable mixture. Bake 35 minutes in medium oven.

Deep-Dish Steak

$3/4$ pound round steak, $1^{1}/_2$ inches thick
$1/4$ cup flour
1 teaspoon salt (optional)
$1/4$ teaspoon pepper
$1^{1}/_2$ tablespoons vegetable oil (or use nonstick cooking spray)
1 medium onion, chopped
1 green pepper, chopped
1 stalk celery, chopped
$1/3$ cup raisins
2 large tomatoes, cut in chunks

Mix flour, salt, and pepper. Rub into steak. Heat oven pan on stove top over medium heat. Add oil and brown meat on both sides. Remove from heat. Add remaining ingredients. Cover and bake in medium oven 1 to $1^{1}/_2$ hours. Turn meat occasionally. Serve with bread.

Don Carlos's Steak Surprise

$3/4$ pound top round steak, cut in thin strips
1 tablespoon olive oil
$1/2$ cup green onion, chopped
1 green pepper, sliced
1 large tomato, chopped
1 clove garlic, minced
1 teaspoon chili powder
$1/2$ teaspoon salt (optional)

In metal baking pan over medium heat on stove top, sauté vegetables in oil until tender. Add meat and brown briefly. Remove from heat. Add seasonings and stir until well coated. Cover and bake in medium oven 35 to 40 minutes.

A Different Sort of Onion

1 large onion, halved, centers removed (reserve for sauce)

$1/4$ pound each ground beef and ground pork

$1/4$ cup salted peanuts, chopped or crushed

$1/4$ teaspoon pepper

$1/8$ teaspoon nutmeg

1 beef bouillon cube

1 cup boiling water

1 15-ounce can whole tomatoes, drained, chopped, and divided in half

Sauce

onion centers

$1/2$ divided tomatoes

$1/4$ cup mushrooms, chopped

2 tablespoons sour cream

2 tablespoons Madeira wine

Cut onion in half and remove center (save), leaving two "cups." Mix beef, pork, nuts, pepper, and nutmeg. Stuff onion halves. Place in 9-by-9-inch baking pan (glass or metal). Dissolve bouillon cube in water, add half of tomatoes, and pour into pan. Bake in medium oven 1 hour. While main dish is cooking, make sauce. Mince onion centers and combine with mushrooms, remaining tomatoes, sour cream, and wine. Heat on stove in small pan. Pour sauce over onion halves before serving.

Merry-Nade Pot Roast

$3/4$ pound chuck steak or small rump or round roast

$1/4$ cup Italian salad dressing

3 tablespoons butter or margarine

$1/2$ cup water

1 large onion, sliced

3 carrots, sliced

2 large potatoes, cut in chunks

2 tablespoons water

1 teaspoon flour

Pour salad dressing over meat. In oven pan over medium flame, melt 2 tablespoons butter, add meat, and brown. Remove from heat and add water and vegetables. Bake in medium oven 1 hour. Remove meat from pan, place pan on stove top, and add 1 tablespoon butter. Whisk flour and water together and stir into sauce to thicken gravy.

Staying Italian for a moment . . .

Katie's Lasagna

8 ounces precooked lasagna noodles (or use the ones that don't need precooking)

$3/4$ pound lean ground beef (95 percent)

$1^1/2$ to 2 cups spaghetti sauce

1 cup ricotta cheese

$1/2$ cup Parmesan cheese (freshly grated is best)

Brown beef in baking pan on stove top over medium heat. Drain and add spaghetti sauce. Remove meat-sauce mixture from pan to bowl. Do not clean pan. Place a single layer of noodles on bottom of pan. Combine cheeses in bowl. Top noodles with layer of cheese, followed by layer of sauce. Repeat until you run out of noodles. Bake uncovered in medium oven 35 to 40 minutes.

Saucy Beef

$3/4$ pound top or bottom round

salt and pepper to taste

$1/4$ cup flour

2 tablespoons prepared mustard

1 tablespoon vegetable oil

1 large onion, diced

2 large potatoes, thinly sliced

1 beef bouillon cube

1 cup boiling water

$1/2$ cup sour cream

Rub flour onto meat. Season with salt and pepper. Rub mustard on meat. Cut meat into bite-size chunks. Heat oil in baking pan or medium casserole and brown meat. Add onions and sauté until tender. Remove from heat and dissolve bouillon cube in water. Pour over meat. Add potatoes. Bake in medium oven 45 minutes. Just before serving, stir in sour cream—this creates an incredible sauce. Serve with fresh carrot sticks and rolls.

Red-Eye Stew

$3/4$ pound stew beef, cut in 1-inch cubes

2 tablespoons butter or margarine

1 large onion, chopped

$1/2$ teaspoon salt (optional)

1 teaspoon paprika

$1/4$ teaspoon caraway seeds

1 6-ounce can tomato paste

1 beef bouillon cube dissolved in 1 cup hot water

2 large potatoes, cubed

In oven pan or casserole on stove top, melt butter over medium heat and brown beef. Reduce heat and sauté onions. Remove from heat and add all ingredients except potatoes. Cover and bake 1 hour in medium oven. Stir in potatoes and cook another 30 minutes. Serve with hard rolls.

Big Ben Beef Bake

¾ pound flank steak
¼ cup honey
¼ cup BBQ sauce
2 tablespoons vegetable oil
2 tablespoons lemon juice
1 large onion, cut in chunks
1 red pepper, sliced

Combine honey, BBQ sauce, oil, and lemon juice to make a sauce. Rub into meat and let it rest in sauce 10 to 15 minutes. Place meat in oven pan and surround with vegetables. Pour any remaining sauce over all. Bake uncovered 15 to 20 minutes in medium to hot oven. Serve with precooked and reheated noodles.

BBQ Brisket

¾ to 1 pound beef brisket
1 cup BBQ sauce
1 large onion, sliced

Rub sauce into meat and let stand 30 minutes. Place in oven pan with onions and sauce. Cover and bake in low to medium oven for 1 to 1½ hours. Slice across grain and serve on hard roll or with rice, accompanied by fresh fruit and some vegetables.

Stepping up your meat selection a notch can bring even more interesting taste variations. By purchasing sirloin, eye of round, and filet, you'll be putting four-star restaurant quality on your cockpit table. You can reduce the fat count by choosing Select cuts. "Select" is a USDA grade that means those cuts have less marbling than "Choice" or "Prime." However, with many oven dishes you may have a better outcome with the fattier pieces because they are less likely to dry out during cooking.

Rib-Eye Ecstasy

2 rib-eye steaks, about $1/2$ pound each
2 tablespoons corn oil
$1/2$ teaspoon each salt (optional) and pepper
1 teaspoon paprika
$1/2$ teaspoon garlic powder
1 large onion, sliced
1 15-ounce can corn, drained

Combine seasonings. Rub both sides of steak with oil and seasonings. Lay onion on bottom of oven pan and place meat on top. Cover and bake in hot oven 20 minutes. After first 15 minutes, spoon corn onto meat. You can add a little steak sauce after cooking, if you like.

———————

Baron Beef

1 pound eye-of-round roast
1 tablespoon vegetable oil
1 tablespoon Kitchen Bouquet Browning and Seasoning Sauce
1 teaspoon each salt (optional), pepper, and thyme

Combine oil and Kitchen Bouquet Sauce. Rub over meat. Mix salt, pepper, and thyme and rub over meat. Place roast in oven pan. Bake 15 minutes in very hot oven. Reduce heat and continue baking for another hour.

☛ *Tip: To complete your meal, wrap some thickly sliced carrots, green onions, and red and green peppers in foil (season with a dash of sesame oil) and add to oven for the last 30 minutes of baking.*

———————

Cap o' Filet (It's the Top!)

2 filets mignons (each about 1$\frac{1}{2}$ inches thick)

2 tablespoons liver pâté

1 tablespoon olive oil

1 teaspoon celery salt (optional)

2 large mushrooms

$\frac{1}{4}$ cup Gruyère cheese, grated

2 tablespoons minced fresh spinach

2 tablespoons seasoned breadcrumbs

1 teaspoon olive oil

2 slices Gruyère cheese ($\frac{1}{4}$ inch thick)

Make a pocket in each filet by cutting into one side; be careful not to cut filets in half. Stuff each cavity with 1 tablespoon of pâté (it should not squirt out past edge). Rub oil on meat and season with celery salt. Set aside. Mix grated cheese, spinach, breadcrumbs, and oil. Remove stem of mushrooms. Carefully cut off part of cap to make flat surface. Stuff mushrooms with cheese mixture. Place meat in oven pan and bake in medium oven about 20 minutes. Place a slice of cheese and a mushroom on top of each filet and continue baking another 10 minutes.

■ PORK, HAM, AND OTHER "OVENABLES"

Sure, you can fry a pork chop or dice up some pork loin and mix it with veggies. But imagine the lip smacking that will ensue when you fire up the oven and make a mess of ribs or a pork roast smothered in applesauce. There are all those interesting variations that put two parts of your kitchen—stove top and oven—to work. (The paella recipes on pages 142–43 are examples of this.) Think about how good your stomach will feel when you wrap yourself around a mouth-watering casserole that highlights ham and cheese. (Remember to cook your pork thoroughly!) Enough imagining; how about some eating?

Cortland Pork Roast

$^3/_4$ pound boneless pork loin roast

1 tablespoon vegetable oil

3 tablespoons brown sugar

1 medium apple, chopped

$^1/_2$ cup applesauce

1 teaspoon cinnamon

1 teaspoon nutmeg

Rub oil and then 1 tablespoon brown sugar onto roast. Bake in a medium oven 45 minutes. Combine apple, applesauce, 2 tablespoons brown sugar, and spices. Spoon over roast. Cover and bake another 45 minutes. Serve with reheated rice and relish tray of pickles, olives, pickled beets, and celery.

———————

Champignon Chops

2 center-cut boneless pork loin chops

1 packet mushroom soup (single-serving size) and water to prepare

parsley, chopped

1 large potato, sliced

In oven pan, brown chops in a little oil. Remove from heat and pour mushroom soup over top. Sprinkle with parsley. Lay potato slices around edge of pan. Cover and bake 45 minutes in medium oven.

———————

"Not the Cold Shoulder" Pork Roast

1 to 1½ pound pork shoulder roast

1 tablespoon (or more) caraway seeds

salt and pepper to taste

1 15-ounce can sauerkraut, drained

Rub spices onto meat. Spread sauerkraut evenly across the bottom of the pan. Place roast on top, cover with foil, and bake in medium oven for 1½ hours. Serve with spiced apple slices. Serves 3 or 4.

Mom's Tuna-Noodle Casserole

2 cups precooked egg noodles

1 tablespoon oil or nonstick cooking spray

1 6-ounce can tuna, drained (or softpack)

1 can condensed mushroom soup

¼ cup parsley, chopped

1 tablespoon butter or margarine, melted

breadcrumbs

In lightly greased casserole, mix tuna, noodles, soup (do not add water), and parsley. Drizzle melted butter over top. Sprinkle breadcrumbs over all. Bake 35 minutes in medium oven.

Italian Sausage Bake-Off

3/4 pound mild Italian sausage

1 15-ounce can tomato sauce

1/2 teaspoon oregano

1/2 teaspoon basil

1/2 teaspoon garlic powder

2 teaspoons sugar

1 bay leaf

1/4 teaspoon fennel seed

2 teaspoons Parmesan cheese

1 large onion, chopped

1 large green pepper, sliced

1 zucchini, sliced

1 large tomato, diced

6 slices provolone cheese

In medium baking pan on stove top, brown sausage over medium heat. In bowl, mix tomato sauce, seasonings, sugar, and Parmesan to make marinara sauce. Remove pan from heat, drain grease, and mix in vegetables. Pour sauce over all. Lay slices of provolone cheese over top and bake in hot oven 35 to 40 minutes. Serve over precooked pasta.

_____

Here's an easy meal that will fill you up.

Big BBQ Ribs

4 farmer-style (with meat on, not spareribs) pork ribs

3/4 cup BBQ sauce

1 large onion, cut in chunks

1 1/2 cups precooked rice

In oven pan, place ribs and smother with BBQ sauce. Pack onion around ribs. Bake in medium oven 45 minutes to 1 hour. About 10 minutes before ribs are done, add rice right on top of the ribs.

_____

Lanai Ground Loin

$^3/_4$ pound ground pork loin

1 tablespoon oil or nonstick cooking spray

$^1/_2$ teaspoon salt (optional)

1 Vidalia (sweet) onion, diced

1 sweet red pepper, diced

$^1/_4$ teaspoon dry mustard

2 eggs, beaten

$^3/_4$ cup breadcrumbs

$^1/_2$ cup crushed pineapple

Combine all ingredients. Turn into lightly greased pie pan and bake in medium oven 45 minutes. Serve hot with freshly sliced cucumbers marinated in white wine vinegar.

Yam 'n' Ham

1 pound smoked shoulder or canned ham

whole cloves

$^1/_3$ cup light brown sugar

2 medium sweet potatoes, quartered

2 tablespoons butter or margarine

Place meat in oven pan. Stud with cloves and sprinkle with brown sugar. Place sweet potatoes around meat, skin side down, and dab with butter. Cover and bake in medium oven 75 minutes. Serve with reheated rice or make beans and rice as a side dish.

Pork Pie (Not the Hat)

    1 package prepared pie crusts (2 crusts)

    2 cups precooked pork loin, diced

    $1/4$ cup bacon bits

    2 large potatoes, thinly sliced

    1 large onion, diced

    1 packet brown gravy mix and 1 cup water to prepare

    salt and pepper to taste

    1 teaspoon sage

Line pie plate with one pie crust. Sprinkle with bacon bits. Layer potatoes and onions. Mix salt, pepper, sage, and pork and make a final layer. Prepare gravy mix and pour gravy over all. Cover with second pie crust. Pinch edges and cut a few vents in top. Bake in medium oven 1 hour.

☛ *Tip: Pork shoulder works well, too, and gives a richer flavor.*

Smokehouse Special

    1 cup ham, diced

    2 medium potatoes, peeled and thinly sliced

    1 medium onion, sliced

    $1/2$ cup cheddar cheese, grated

    $1/2$ cup milk

    2 tablespoons flour

    2 to 3 tablespoons breadcrumbs

In baking pan on stove top, heat milk to near boiling. Gradually add cheese and flour to make sauce, whisking to avoid lumps. Remove from heat and stir in ham, potatoes, and onions. Sprinkle breadcrumbs over the top and bake in medium oven 45 minutes.

■ BAKED GOODS

Home baking in the 21st century sometimes seems to be a dying art. People still want the taste and texture of freshly baked breads, rolls, and biscuits. They just think that the work involved and the skills required are beyond them. Truth is, baking is not as hard as you might think. We'll admit pastries are more difficult, but there's nothing easier than making some hot biscuits to take the edge off an early-morning start down the Waterway.

A lot of the prepackaged rolls you can buy will keep a day or two without overt refrigeration. Simply pack the cylinder near frozen meat or a bag of ice in your cooler or icebox to keep chilled until you're ready to bake the rolls. Then follow package instructions.

If you're a bit more ambitious, you can start from scratch. Here are a couple of our favorites.

Hi-Ho Cornbread

1^1/$_2$ cups flour
^{2}/$_3$ cup yellow cornmeal
4 tablespoons sugar
salt (optional)
2 teaspoons baking powder
2 eggs, beaten
1 cup milk
4 tablespoons vegetable oil

Mix dry ingredients. Add wet ingredients, stirring to mix batter evenly. Pour batter in greased 9-inch square pan and bake 25 minutes in a hot oven. Check with straw or toothpick for doneness and make sure bread doesn't burn.

———————

Confetti Cornbread

To Hi-Ho Cornbread recipe, add ^{1}/$_4$ cup diced red pepper, ^{1}/$_4$ cup diced green pepper, and 1 teaspoon minced fresh cilantro. You can also stir in ^{1}/$_4$ cup of grated cheddar cheese. Add 10 to 15 minutes to cooking time to account for additional moisture from veggies.

———————

This next recipe works great in a frying pan, too. Simply cook the patties 2 to 3 minutes per side or until browned.

Big D's Biscuits

   1 cup flour
   1 teaspoon baking powder
   pinch of salt (optional)
   1 teaspoon vegetable oil
   $^1/_2$ cup water

Combine all ingredients, adding just enough water to make a good stiff dough. Flour your hands and form biscuits about 2 inches in diameter and 1 inch thick. Place on greased oven pan. Bake 10 to 15 minutes in a medium oven, checking to see that biscuits don't burn.

Hush My Puppies

   1 cup yellow cornmeal
   $^1/_2$ teaspoon salt (optional)
   $^1/_2$ teaspoon baking powder
   1 egg, beaten
   $^1/_2$ cup milk
   1 tablespoon onion, minced
   1 tablespoon vegetable oil

Combine dry ingredients. Add egg, milk, and onion. Mix together to form dough. Shape into $^1/_2$-inch oblong patties and place on greased oven pan or cookie sheet. Brush tops with oil and bake in hot oven 10 to 15 minutes or until nicely browned.

Pam's Special "Things"

shortening or oil
2 cups biscuit mix
$^2/_3$ cup milk
1 tablespoon flour
3 tablespoons brown sugar
1 tablespoon cinnamon
$^1/_2$ cup chopped nuts
$^1/_2$ cup raisins
2 tablespoons butter

In mixing bowl, combine biscuit mix and milk. Cut a 12-by-18-inch piece of wax paper. Place on cutting board and sprinkle lightly with flour. Place dough on wax paper and roll into a 8-by-14-inch rectangle, about $^1/_4$ inch thick. Spread brown sugar evenly on the dough, then sprinkle with cinnamon, nuts, and raisins. Put small bits of butter on top. Roll up the dough lengthwise. Use the wax paper to lift dough and help roll. Cut the roll into $^1/_4$- to $^3/_4$-inch slices. Arrange slices on greased cookie sheet. Put pan in medium (350°F) oven. Cook for 15 to 20 minutes until browned.

Shortcake Biscuits

1 cup flour
$1^1/_2$ teaspoons baking powder
$1^1/_2$ tablespoons sugar
$^1/_4$ teaspoon salt (optional)
1 egg, beaten
$^1/_3$ cup milk
2 tablespoons vegetable oil

Combine all ingredients. Dough should be stiff. If it seems too loose, add some flour. Coat hands with flour and form biscuits about $^1/_2$ to $^3/_4$ inch thick and 3 inches across. Bake in hot oven 15 minutes.

DESSERT

Do you like dessert? The oven is the way to go for after-dinner tasties. Any cake mix will do for starters, and brownies fill you up after a long day in the cockpit. And all of those come in prepackaged, ready-to-go form. Just visit the baking aisle at your store. And, if you're daring, you can build your dessert from scratch.

Remember that you have to watch the oven temperature or else you might end up with a charred "might-have-been." Test for doneness by sticking a toothpick into the middle of the cake. If it comes out clean, the cake is done.

Powerful Gingerbread

$1/4$ cup butter or margarine

$1/4$ cup sugar

1 egg, beaten

1 cup flour

$1/2$ teaspoon baking soda

$1/2$ teaspoon cinnamon

$1/2$ teaspoon ginger

$1/4$ teaspoon ground cloves

$1/4$ teaspoon salt (optional)

$1/3$ cup molasses

$1/2$ cup hot water

$1/4$ cup raisins

Cream butter and sugar in a bowl with a fork. Mix in egg. Combine dry ingredients in a cup or bowl. Mix molasses and hot water in a cup. Alternate adding dry ingredients and molasses mixture to sugar and egg. Beat until smooth. Stir in raisins. Pour into greased 8-inch round cake pan and bake in medium oven for about 45 minutes.

Apple Heaven

2 medium apples (McIntosh are best), thinly sliced
2 tablespoons brown sugar
2 teaspoons butter or margarine
$1/2$ teaspoon cinnamon
$1/2$ teaspoon nutmeg

Place apples in 8-inch round pan. Sprinkle with brown sugar and spices and place dots of butter all around. Cover and bake in medium oven 20 minutes.

Apple-Cinnamon Coffee Cake

$1^1/2$ cups Bisquick
$1/2$ cup applesauce
$1/4$ cup brown sugar
2 teaspoons cinnamon
$1/4$ cup milk
1 egg, beaten

Topping

$1/2$ cup brown sugar
2 tablespoons butter or margarine

To make cake, lightly mix brown sugar, cinnamon, applesauce, milk, and egg. Gradually add Bisquick until you have a smooth batter. Pour into greased cake pan. To make topping, use a fork to cream topping ingredients together until crumbly. Sprinkle over top of batter. Bake in medium oven 25 minutes or until center of coffee cake is done.

Blue-Tooth Cobbler

$^1/_2$ cup fresh blueberries (substitute apples, thinly sliced, if desired)

$^1/_2$ teaspoon cinnamon

$^1/_4$ teaspoon nutmeg

$^1/_2$ teaspoon flour

1 cup Bisquick

2 tablespoons butter or margarine

$^1/_4$ cup sugar

1 egg, beaten

$^1/_2$ cup milk

In greased oven pan, combine blueberries, spices, and flour. In bowl, mix all other ingredients and pour over fruit mixture. Bake in medium oven 25 minutes or until top is browned. Turn out upside down onto serving platter.

———————

Oops, I Flipped the Pineapple Cake Upside Down!

2 tablespoons vegetable oil

$^1/_3$ cup brown sugar

1 8-ounce can sliced pineapple, drained

1 9-ounce box Jiffy yellow cake mix

1 egg, beaten (substitute 2 tablespoons whole egg powder, if desired)

$^1/_2$ cup water (if you use egg powder, add 3 tablespoons water)

In 9-inch cake pan, swirl oil until bottom of pan is covered. Mix brown sugar into oil, creating an even layer that covers only the bottom of the pan. Lay pineapple on the sugar. Set aside. In bowl, mix the cake mix and egg until fully blended. Add water and beat for 3 to 4 minutes. Pour evenly over fruit and sugar. Set Outback Oven on top of stove. Heat over medium-to-high flame until temperature indicator reaches Bake. Cook for 25 minutes, adjusting flame as needed.

☛ Tip: In a built-in oven, set to medium heat and cook for 25 to 30 minutes.

———————

THE OVEN • DESSERT

Twoti-Fruiti Pie

1 package prepared pie crusts (2 crusts)
$^1/_2$ cup blueberries
$^3/_4$ cup apples, thinly sliced
$^1/_4$ cup sugar
$^1/_2$ teaspoon cinnamon
$^1/_4$ teaspoon nutmeg
1 teaspoon flour
1 tablespoon butter or margarine

Place one pie crust in bottom of pie plate. In bowl, mix all other ingredients except butter. Pour onto crust. Dot top of filling with butter and cover with top crust. Pinch edges and cut vents in top. Sprinkle top crust with a few drops of water. Bake in medium oven 45 minutes.

☞ *Tip: Use this recipe to make apple pie; just omit the blueberries and double the amount of apples.*

Appendix

■ WEIGHTS & MEASURES

weight
1 ounce = 28.35 grams
1 pound = 16 ounces = 453.6 grams
2.2 pounds = 1 kilogram

volume
1 teaspoon = 5 milliliters
1 tablespoon = 3 teaspoons = 15 milliliters
1 fluid ounce = 6 teaspoons = $\frac{1}{8}$ cup = 29.56 milliliters
1 cup = 16 tablespoons = 8 fluid ounces = 236 milliliters
1 pint = 16 fluid ounces = 2 cups = 0.5 liter
1 quart = 32 fluid ounces = 2 pints = 0.9 liter
1 gallon = 128 fluid ounces = 4 quarts = 3.8 liters

length
1 inch = 2.54 centimeters

thermometer
To convert:
(°F–32) x 0.555 = °C
(°C x 1.8) + 32 = °F

slow oven = 300–325°F (150–165°C)
medium oven = 350–375°F (175–185°C)
hot oven = 400–425°F (205–220°C)

■ SAMPLE MENU FORM

DAY 1 _____   **PAGE #**

dinner

_____   _____

_____   _____

_____   _____

DAY 2 _____

breakfast

_____   _____

_____   _____

_____   _____

lunch

_____   _____

_____   _____

_____   _____

dinner

_____   _____

_____   _____

_____   _____

DAY 3 _____

breakfast

_____   _____

_____   _____

_____   _____

lunch

_____   _____

_____   _____

_____   _____

Choosing a menu is a personal thing, and your tastes may not be the same as ours. But we've chosen a menu for a week that reflects our tastes to illustrate how easy it is to eat well on your cruise with just a little extra effort.

We've only chosen recipes for breakfast and dinner, plus a few for desserts. (Remember, all recipes make two servings unless otherwise indicated.) Our assumption is that you, like us, would prefer to keep lunches simple. A quick sandwich, for example, with perhaps some soup (from a can or softpack) to warm you up.

Our sample menu includes recipes made with a frying pan, a pot, and baked in the oven. Depending on how "cool" you are (refrigerator or icebox), you may want to eat the chicken meals first and save the beef for the end of the trip. In any case, follow our suggestions in chapter 2 for freezing meat for your cruise.

So, as we said earlier, *bon appetit!*

Breakfast

Day 1: Eggs à la Haifa
(see page 40)

Day 2: Flor-Egg-Enzo
(see pages 40–41)

Day 3: Oatmeal Extraordinaire
(see page 81)

Day 4: Rasher Cake
(see page 134)

Day 5: Omelet à la Terry Rodriguez
(see page 43)

Day 6: Amsterdam Apple Pancake
(see page 133)

Day 7: Eggs à la Goldenrod
(see page 86)

Dinner

Day 1: Sticky Chicken
(see page 52)

Day 2: Poulet Pie
(see page 140)

Day 3: Big King Chicken Casserole
(see page 139)

Day 4: Chicken Papri-Crash (see page 53)

Day 5: Garibaldi's Roast Beef (see page 112)

Day 6: Very Green Stuffed Peppers
(see page 105)

Day 7: Bangkok Beef 'n' Peppers
(see pages 72–73)

Dessert

Oops, I Flipped the Pineapple Cake Upside Down!
(see page 169)

Fruit Compote
(see page 129)

Trifle (see page 127)

Blue-Tooth Cobbler
(see page 169)

PROVISIONING

There's said to be more than one way to skin a cat, and the same holds true for provisioning. John and Susan's first experience provisioning for more than a weekend involved following the instructor for their one-week cruising school charter through a grocery store while he pulled seemingly random items from the shelves. The whole process was somewhat chaotic even if it was based on the instructor's experience.

But if you want to eat well—and by that we mean eating delicious meals—you've got to put some thought into it. Making up a menu is the first step, and then compose your shopping list, as we've done here.

WEEKLONG MENU SHOPPING LIST

Provisions (staples)

milk (4¼ cups)

flour (1¼ cups)

cornstarch (2 tsp.)

baking powder
(1 tsp.)

salt

pepper (black and white)

sugar (1 cup brown,
¾ cup white)

Carbs

French or Italian
bread (1 small loaf)

your favorite bread
(4 slices)

seasoned bread-
crumbs (½ cup+)

Bisquick (1⅔ cups)

white cornmeal
(½ cup)

rice (1½ cups
precooked)

wild rice (1 cup
precooked)

Minute Rice
(½ cup uncooked,
¾ cup precooked)

oatmeal (⅔ cup)

Jiffy yellow cake
mix (9 oz. box)

prepared pie crusts
(2)

Twinkies (2)

Proteins

peanut butter
(¼ cup)

eggs (26 to 27)

bacon (6 strips)

rump or round
roast (½ to ¾ lb.)

sirloin (¾ lb.)

sliced salami
(¼ lb.)

chicken breasts
(5, about ½ lb. ea.;
or equivalent in soft-
packs or cans)

grated cheddar
cheese (6 oz.)

grated Parmesan
cheese (3 tbsp.)

Vegetables/Fruits

strawberries or
blueberries (¾ cup)

blueberries or
apple (½ cup)

apples (2)

lemon juice (1 tbsp.)

peach (1)

mandarin oranges
(6 oz. can)

sliced pineapple
(8 oz. can)

dried apricots
(½ cup)

raisins (¾ cup)

green peppers
(2 large, 2 medium,
1 small)

red peppers
(2 medium)

sliced pimiento
pepper (4 oz. jar)

carrots (2 medium)

celery (2 stalks)

sliced mushrooms
(1 cup)

onions (2 large,
7 medium)

potatoes (1 large,
3 medium)

tomatoes (2 large,
1 medium)

frozen peas (1 cup)

garlic (1 clove)

Fats/Oils

olive oil (6 tbsp.)

peanut oil
(2⅓ tbsp.)

vegetable oil
(4 tbsp.)

butter or margarine
(6 tbsp.)

pimento-stuffed
olives (6 oz. jar)

walnuts (¼ cup)

Sweeteners/Spices

ketchup (1 tbsp.)

mustard (2 tbsp.)

soy sauce (3 tbsp.)

honey (1 tbsp.)

beef bouillon cube
(1)

chicken bouillon
cubes (2)

chicken gravy
(1 oz. packet or
1 small can)

basil (½ tsp.)

cayenne pepper
(¾ tsp.)

garlic powder
(1 tsp.)

paprika (1 tbsp.)

cinnamon (1 tsp.)

ginger (½ tsp.)

nutmeg (¼ tsp.)

■ NUTRITIONAL CONTENT OF SOME COMMON FOODS

FOOD	KILOCALORIES PER 3½ OUNCES	% FAT	% PROTEIN	% CARBO-HYDRATE
Dairy products, fats, and oils				
margarine	720	81.0	0.6	0.4
low-fat spread	366	36.8	6.0	3.0
vegetable oil	900	100.0	–	–
instant dried skim milk	355	1.3	36.0	53.0
cheddar cheese	398	32.2	25.0	2.1
Edam cheese	305	23.0	24.0	–
Parmesan cheese	410	30.0	35.0	–
eggs, dried	592	41.2	47.0	4.1
low-fat cheese spread	175	9.0	20.0	4.0
Dried fruit				
apples	275	–	1.0	78.0
apricots	261	–	5.0	66.5
dates	275	–	2.2	72.9
figs	275	–	4.3	69.1
peaches	261	–	3.1	68.3
raisins	289	–	2.5	77.4
Vegetables				
potatoes, dehydrated	352	–	8.3	80.4
tomato flakes	342	–	10.8	76.7
baked beans	123	2.6	6.1	19.0
Nuts				
almonds	600	57.7	18.6	19.5
Brazil nuts	652	66.9	14.3	10.9
coconut, desiccated	605	62.0	6.0	6.0
peanut butter	589	49.4	27.8	17.2
peanuts, roasted	582	49.8	26.0	18.8
Grains				
oatmeal	375	7.0	11.0	62.4
muesli, sweetened	348	6.3	10.4	66.6
pasta, white	370	–	12.5	75.2

FOOD	KILOCALORIES PER 3½ OUNCES	% FAT	% PROTEIN	% CARBO-HYDRATE
Grains (cont.)				
pasta, whole wheat	323	0.5	12.5	67.2
rice, brown	359	—	7.5	77.4
rice, white	363	—	6.7	80.4
flour, plain	360	2.0	11.0	75.0
flour, wholemeal	345	3.0	12.0	72.0
Baked products				
granola bar	382	13.4	4.9	64.4
crispbread, rye	345	1.2	13.0	76.3
oat crackers	369	15.7	10.1	65.6
bread, white	271	—	8.7	50.5
bread, wholemeal	243	—	10.5	47.7
cookies, chocolate	525	28.0	6.0	67.0
fig bar	356	5.6	3.9	75.4
cake, fruit	355	13.0	5.0	58.0
Meat and fish				
beef, dried	204	6.3	34.3	—
beef, corned, canned	264	18.0	23.5	—
salami	490	45.0	19.0	2.0
salmon, canned	151	7.1	20.8	—
sardines, drained	165	11.1	24.0	—
tuna, drained	165	8.2	28.8	—
Sugars and sweets				
honey	303	—	0.3	82.0
sugar, brown	373	—	—	96.4
sugar, white	384	—	—	99.5
chocolate, milk	518	32.3	7.7	56.9
custard, instant	378	10.2	2.9	72.6
Drinks				
cocoa (mix)	391	10.6	9.4	73.9
coffee	2	—	0.2	—
tea	1	—	0.1	—

Adapted from Agricultural Handbook No. 8: Composition of Foods (U.S. Department of Agriculture); Food Facts by David Briggs and Mark Wahlquist; and manufacturer's specifications. Courtesy of The Backpacker's Handbook by Chris Townsend (Ragged Mountain Press, 1997).

Index

Numbers in **bold** refer to pages with photographs.